C#

An Ultimate Beginner's Guide to C#

Liam Damien

Table of Contents

v

Introduction

C# programming language is introduced by Microsoft with the intention of keeping object oriented programming language as simple, modern and general purpose. Microsoft developed C# language on the basis of several other languages mainly Java and C++. C# is a machine code which mainly runs with .Net framework and used for building .Net applications. Visual Studio IDE (Integrated development environment) is the best tool to build programs in C#.

C# is a Component Oriented Programming language. With C#, you can define software components and attach these to different software products, just like an engine is used in a car or a bike. Therefore, components are interchangeable and reusable. For example, we can use the calendar component in any application browser that we build and also in Microsoft Office.

C# offers Type safety by preventing programs from accessing memory outside the bounds of an object's public properties. With .NET Framework's smart Garbage Collection, we need not worry about unused objects. These are removed automatically by the framework.

When we write code in C#, we write everything in one place. There is no need for header files, Interface Definition Language or IDL files, Globally Unique Identifiers or GUID's and complicated interfaces. We can embed our software and host it in various environments. This is a standalone addition only in C#.

In most other programming languages, every datatype is unique on its own and is not derived from any other type. But in C#, every pre-defined as well as user-defined datatype is derived from a special reference type called an object. So, if you have an object o, you can assign a value of 38 or 859.16 or Hello to o.

Structure of a C # Program

```
using System;
using System.Collections.Generic;
using System.Linq;

namespace MyProgram
{
    class Program
    {
        static void Main(string[] args)
        {

        Console.WriteLine("This is my First C# Program");

        }
    }
}
```

Explanation

The above program is a sample console program.

Using Statement

We write the using statement at the very start of our program to make use of the all the classes and objects functionalities in the c sharp library. By including using System; statement can avoid the usage of system namespace in the program i.e. System.Console.WriteLine(""); can be return as Console.WriteLine("");

Example:

```
using System;
using System.Data;
using System.Data.SqlClient;
```

Features of C# Programming Language

C# implements many features to offer a complete programming language. Let us look at the advantage of programming with objects. As shown in the below figure (Fig1), to define a car object, we can have a car class with fields like fuel capacity, number of doors and some functions say applyBrake, applyColor and accelerate. This car class behaves as a template to build various objects. The advantage of declaring such a class is that we can create several car objects from the class.

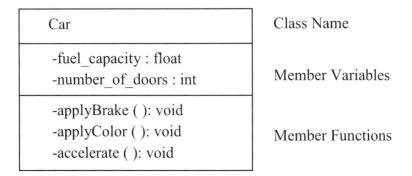

Car	Class Name
-fuel_capacity : float -number_of_doors : int	Member Variables
-applyBrake ( ): void -applyColor ( ): void -accelerate ( ): void	Member Functions

Fig 1: Class with its member variables and member functions

Unlike in any other programming language, where you need to write many functions for different datatypes, you can define a function mySampleFunction which returns a void and pass an object o. This function can be called with an int, double, string or any other user-defined datatype as shown below.

```
void mySampleFunction (float s)
{
//define function here
}
Void mySampleFunction (double s)
{
//define function here
}
Void mySampleFunction (int s)
{
//define function here
}
Void mySampleFunction (string s)
{
//define function here
}
```

We need not follow the above method of writing code; instead we can follow the method below:

```
void mySampleFunction (object o)
{
//define function here
}
mySampleFunction (5);
mySampleFunction (62.75);
mySampleFunction ("Hello");
```

Some of the features of Object Orient Programming are Encapsulation, Polymorphism and Inheritance. Encapsulation binds the data into a single unit and the data is hidden from other classes in the program.

In inheritance, a class will have subclasses which are more specialized versions of a class. From the class car, we can have a subclass called mileage cars from which a mileage car is derived. From the main class, other subclasses like sports car and electric car can be derived.

Polymorphism means a situation where one name may exhibit different behaviors. So when the accelerate function is called by different classes, their performance varies. Mileage car would accelerate up to 80kmph, sports car would accelerate up to 150kmph and an electric car would accelerate up to 100kmph.

Chapter 1

Namespace in C#

As the name suggests, the using directive refers to using an existing namespace. Here, the program is using 'System' which is a namespace defined in .NET Framework and is a keyword. So, what are namespaces?

Namespaces provide a way to uniquely identify a type and provide logical organization of types.

Before we proceed to knowing what namespaces are, let's learn the need for them. XYZ is one of the biggest coffee retail outlets in the world. They sell about 20,000 cups of coffee each day. A program to find the sales for the day in three different countries would have prompted the programmer to write three different classes, in three different header files. When the overall sales of the company have to be calculated, the headers will have to be merged. In such a case, an identifier clash is bound to occur as all three branches have a class called Sales_for_the_day. Now in C#, the identifier clash can be easily avoided by using namespaces.

All the classes are defined under namespaces Singapore, England, and India respectively. On integration, all three objects obj1, obj2 and obj3 are created and there is no identifier clash.

Namespaces can be nested. Suppose our destination was to reach the State of Texas within the USA (country), which itself belongs to the continent NA? Then we will have to access all the countries inside NA by the using NA directive. Then, to access all the cities within USA, we use the using NA.USA directive and, to access Texas, we use the using NA.USA.Texas directive. The general syntax for using an existing namespace is, using outer namespace followed by an optional .inner namespace. The general syntax for defining namespace is as shown below:

General syntax for using namespaces:
> using outernamespace[.innernamespace];

General syntax for defining namespaces:
> namespace identifier
> { [namespace identifier()] }
> [] -> denotes optional

It is hard to remember such a huge list of namespaces. Hence C# allows us to create custom alias names. So instead of using outernamespace.innernamespace, we can call it as 'test' with the simple statement using space test equals

outernamespace.innernamespace, thereby avoiding reuse of long and confusing names for nested namespaces. This denotes we are defining a namespace MyNameSpace. Therefore, the general syntax to define a namespace is as seen below:

```
using test = outernamespace.innernamespace;
namespace identifier
{
// all type definitions
}
```

So what is valid? Can we just give some name of our convenience? Of course we can but there are some limitations, as follows:

Rule1: No spaces in between.

Rule 2: Begins with underscore, @, A to Z or a to z – it is case sensitive.

Rule 3: Do not use a keyword of C# such as using, if and namespace; instead prefix with @ or underscore. Example: @using and _using.

There may be some cases however, where we may forget the namespaces created by us. For such cases, we use global, followed by a scope resolution operator to recollect the pre-defined namespaces as **global:**

Important Points about Namespaces

- Namespaces in C# are compilation units that let us to organize and reuse code which gets exposed for use to remaining modules of programs.

- Inside a namespace, you are free to declare any other namespace, structure, interface, class, delegate or enumeration.

- Defining items such as variables, events, and properties is not allowed. They need to be explicitly declared in the class itself.

- Namespaces can be nested i.e. we can use namespaces inside another namespaces

- Namespaces can also avoid ambiguity in the program, which means that we write large numbers of code lines and they may contain many classes and code elements

- So if we group the code blocks that have logical hierarchy under one space, we can organize the program properly. We can refer to the code elements under a particular name space by using statement.

Example:

Suppose a program has a namespace structure like below

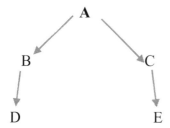

We can refer to the code elements in D and E namespaces as follows:

using A.B.D;
using A.C.E;

Naming Conventions in C#

- Namespace, Class and method names should start with a Capital letter and the starting letter of each word in name should be capitalized.

- Variable names should start with a lowercase letter and the starting letter of each word in a name should be capitalized. We can also include '_' before the name declaration.

Let us first see a very simple program in C#.

Simple C# Program using Namespaces

We now have a basic understanding of the various features of a C# program. Let us look at this simple C# program shown below.

```
// file named as 'Class1.cs'
using System;
namespace MyNameSpace
{
        class Hello
        {
                static void Main (string[] args)
                {
                        Console.WriteLine ("Hello World");
                // used for single line comment and /* for multiline */
                }
        }
}
```

As we can see, the using System denotes that we are using the pre-defined namespace system. A namespace called MyNameSpace is created, and a class named Hello is defined under it. The method called Main is the entry point to our program. The program runs fine when we give the Main method public access, but since the Main method is the entry point of our program, it should not be called explicitly.

The Main method is called explicitly only if it is given public access and, in such a case, a System.StackOverflowException will be thrown. Therefore, the Main method must be static and it should not be public.

The Console.WriteLine method under the Console class defined in the System namespace represents the standard input, output and error streams for Console Applications.

After we type this program in the editor, invoke the compiler by entering the command csc Hello.cs in the command prompt. Let us see the compilation process. The outcome of this compilation is that the source code is converted into MSIL (Microsoft Intermediate Language). After successfully compiling the source code, we now need to run this program. To run this program, type Hello and press enter. MSIL code is again compiled by the JIT (just in time) compiler and it generates the native code. This native code is executed by the machine's processor. So we can see Hello World on the console.

Chapter 2

OOPS in C#

It comprises of the following topics.

- ➤ **Class**
- ➤ **Name Space**
- ➤ **Method Main**
- ➤ **Types**
- ➤ **Method**
- ➤ **Static Method**
- ➤ **Polymorphism**
- ➤ **Overloading methods**
- ➤ **Method Hiding**
- ➤ **Method Overriding**
- ➤ **Constructor**
- ➤ **Static Constructor**

Introduction

Hello World

The first assignment for any of the C# .net learners will be writing a "Hello World" program. Let us proceed the same way.

Hello World is a program which involves the concepts of class. The below is a C# code.

```
using System;
using System.Collections.Generic;
using System.Linq;
using System.Text;
namespace OOPSConcepts
{
    class HelloWorld
    {
        static void Main(string[] args)
        {
            Console.WriteLine("Hello World");
            Console.ReadLine();
        }
    }
}
```

```
Hello World
```

Class

A class is a combination of related methods and variables. It describes them. Instances of the classes could be made to describe the methods and the variables. We can create many instances of the class depending upon the requirement.

The default access modifier of Class is Internal. Class comprises all the data members. (Methods, variables, constructors, etc.)

Class can be inherited or instantiated depending upon the requirement and usage.

The word **"HelloWorld"** is the name of the class.

Key Word **CLASS** followed by a space and the name of the CLASS.

It is followed by a pair of curly braces.

All the code for your class goes inside these curly brackets.

Namespace

Namespaces are used to organize its large code projects. In the Hello World example, we have seen the usage of "USING SYSTEM"

That means SYSTEM is namespace and one of its class is CONSOLE. As Console is already present in the SYSTEM namespace need not write SYSTEM.CONSOLE and can be written as CONSOLE.

In the Hello World example, we have seen the usage of key word **NAMESPACE.**

These are user defined namespaces. It helps in the limitation of the scope of the class and method names in the large projects. Namespaces can span across another namespace.

Key word **NAMESPACE** followed by space and the name of the namespace (OOPSConcepts) which is appended by the curly braces.

The class (HelloWorld) goes inside the curly braces.

MAIN Method

The starting point of any of the application is the method Main. It is also the ending point. In another way it is the entry and exit point of the application.

It is always static and can have return types as void or int. The Main method should be inside a class or a structure.

The Main method can be declared with or without parameters.

The Main method is the place where the creation of object takes place and also invoking of the other methods happen here.

Example:

```
class HelloWorld
    {
        static void Main(string[] args)
        {
            Console.WriteLine("Hello World");
            Console.ReadLine();
        }
    }
```

Types

Types are of two forms: 1. Value Types and 2. Reference Types

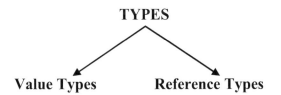

Example:

Value Type:

int iValue = 5;

Reference Type:

String strName = "Anupam";

Value types are further classified as:

1. Simple Types
2. Enums and
3. Structures

Reference types are further classified as:

1. Classes
2. Interfaces
3. Arrays
4. Delegates

Value type is stored in the heap whereas Reference type is stored in the stack.

Value type initialization is 0 whereas for reference type it is NULL.

Value type copies the value whereas reference type copies the reference.

Method

Here is a code example.

```
using System;
using System.Collections.Generic;
using System.Linq;
using System.Text;
namespace OOPSConcepts
{
    class MainClass
    {
        public void Student()
        {
            int noOfStudents = 50;
            Console.WriteLine("No of Students in the Class is " +
            noOfStudents);
        }
        static void Main(string[] args)
        {
            MainClass objMainClass = new MainClass();
            objMainClass.Student();
            Console.ReadLine();
        }
    }
}
```

Output:

```
No of Students in the Class is 50
```

The highlighted part is an example of Method (Student). The access specifier for the method (Student) is **PUBLIC**.

Different access modifiers are: Public, Private, Protected and Internal.

We have created an object inside the Main method to instantiate the class.

Here a method Student() has been created. An object of the class MainClass has been created. With the help of the object we are accessing the method.

The output here would be **No of Students in the Class is 50**

Static Method

Here is an example.

```
using System;
using System.Collections.Generic;
using System.Linq;
using System.Text;
namespace OOPSConcepts
{
    class MainClass
    {
        static void Student()
        {
            int noOfStudents = 50;
            Console.WriteLine("No of Students in the Class is " +
            noOfStudents);
        }
        static void Main(string[] args)
        {
            Student();
            Console.ReadLine();
        }
    }
}
```

Output:

```
No of Students in the Class is 50
```

The method called Student is marked as Static.

Hence we can access the method without creating an object of the class.

Outside the class we need to access the method by using <Class Name>.<Method Name>. Here it will be MainClass.Student().

Example to access a static method which is outside the same class.

To access any method outside the class we should have the access specifier as Public (could be protected, protected internal, but not private).

In the "NewClass" we are calling the method "Student" by using **MainClass.Student()**

```csharp
using System;
using System.Collections.Generic;
using System.Linq;
using System.Text;
namespace OOPSConcepts
{
    class MainClass
    {
        public static void Student()
        {
            int noOfStudents = 50;
            Console.WriteLine("No of Students in the Class is " +
            noOfStudents);
        }

    }
    class NewClass
    {
        static void Main(string[] args)
        {
            MainClass.Student();
            Console.ReadLine();
        }
    }
}
```

Output:

```
No of Students in the Class is 50
```

22

Polymorphism

Polymorphism means, quite literally, many forms. When a message can be processed in different ways then it is called polymorphism.

It allows us to invoke methods of the derived class during run time using the base class reference.

It also allows for implementing the methods with different signatures but called by the same name.

It is of two types:

1. Overriding

2. Overloading

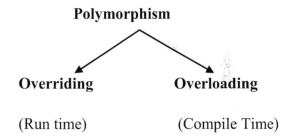

Polymorphism

Overriding

(Run time)

Overloading

(Compile Time)

OVERLOADING METHODS

Overloading is a way of using the operators "+" and "_". The main objective is to use the same class to explain the various parameters of that class.

Here we have multiple methods in the same scope with the same name but different signatures.

One fine example is of a Class Student. For the same Class we can get the count of female students and also the count of all the students.

EXAMPLE

```
using System;
using System.Collections.Generic;
using System.Linq;
using System.Text;
namespace OOPSConcepts
{
    class MainClass
    {
        public void Student(int i)
        {
            Console.WriteLine(i);
        }
        public void Student(int i, int j)
        {
            i = 50;
            j = 50;
            Console.WriteLine(i + j);
        }
    }
    class NewClass
    {
        static void Main(string[] args)
        {
            int i = 0 ;
            int j = 0 ;
            MainClass newObj1 = new MainClass ();
```

```
            newObj1.Student (i);
            MainClass newObj2 = new MainClass ();
            newObj2.Student(i, j);
            Console.ReadLine();
        }
    }
}
```

Output:

Overloading means there are two methods with the same name but the signature changes. While compiling, the compiler chooses which method to use depending upon the call with the arguments.

In the above example there are two methods with the same name, "Student". But only the signature varies. **That is, the first method has int i and the second method has int i, int j**

While calling, objects of the class are created and arguments are passed to call the respective methods.

Method Hiding

Here is an example.

```csharp
using System;
using System.Collections.Generic;
using System.Linq;
using System.Text;
namespace OOPSConcepts
{
    class ClassRoom
    {
    public void classRoomMethod ()
    {
        Console .WriteLine ("I Am inside the Parent Class");
    }
    }
    class child : ClassRoom
    {

        new public void classRoomMethod()
        {
            Console.WriteLine("I am inside the child class");
        }
    }
    class NewClass
    {
        static void Main(string[] args)
        {
            child objChild = new child ();
            objChild.classRoomMethod();
            Console.ReadLine();
        }
    }
}
```

Output:

```
I am inside the child class
```

When we try to hide the functionality of the base class in the derive class, then we use the **NEW** key word in the child class.

This gives completely a new definition to the derived class.

METHOD OVERRIDING

Overriding is a way by which the functionality of the child class can be modified.

```
using System;
using System.Collections.Generic;
using System.Linq;
using System.Text;
namespace OOPSConcepts
{
    class ClassRoom
    {
    public virtual void classRoomMethod ()
    {
        Console .WriteLine ("I Am inside the Parent Class");
    }
    }
    class child : ClassRoom
    {
```

```
        public override void classRoomMethod()
        {
            Console.WriteLine("I am inside the child class");
        }
    }
    class NewClass
    {
        static void Main(string[] args)
        {
            ClassRoom objClassRoom = new ClassRoom();
            objClassRoom.classRoomMethod();
            child objChild = new child ();
            objChild.classRoomMethod();
            Console.ReadLine();


        }
    }
}
```

Output:

```
I Am inside the Parent Class
I am inside the child class
```

When we try to modify the functionality of base class in the derive class then we use the **OVERRIDE** key word in the child class and the **VIRTUAL** key word in the base class for each respective method.

Constructor

```csharp
using System;
using System.Collections.Generic;
using System.Linq;
using System.Text;
namespace OOPSConcepts
{
    class ClassRoom
    {

        string text = "I have apples each costing RS";
        public ClassRoom (int i)
        {
         Console .WriteLine (text + ' ' + i );
        }
    }
    class MainClass
    {
        static void Main(string[] args)
        {
            ClassRoom newObj = new ClassRoom(10);
            Console.ReadLine();

        }
    }
}
```

Output:

```
I have apples each costing RS 10
```

29

The constructor has the same name as the class. A constructor is used to initialize the class members

If there is no constructor, then the compiler creates a default constructor. If there is a constructor declared, then the compiler does not create any default constructors.

STATIC CONSTRUCTOR

```
using System;
using System.Collections.Generic;
using System.Linq;
using System.Text;
namespace OOPSConcepts
{
    class ClassRoom
    {
        public ClassRoom()
        {
            Console.WriteLine("After static constructor in the same
class");
        }
        static ClassRoom ()
        {
        Console .WriteLine("Inside the Static Constructor" );
        }
    }
    class MainClass
    {
        static void Main(string[] args)
        {
            ClassRoom newObj = new ClassRoom();
```

```
            Console.WriteLine("In the main Class");
            Console.ReadLine();

     }
   }
}
```

Output:

```
Inside the Static Constructor
After static constructor in the same class
In the main Class
```

A static constructor should have the same name as the class. It should be parameterless and it shouldn't have any modifiers. It is invoked once before the type is used for the first time. There should only be one static constructor per class.

Chapter 3

Type Conversions in C#

Value Types and Reference Types

Types come in two flavors, namely Value types and Reference types. Value type variables hold the actual value and are allocated in a portion of memory called the stack.

```
int x =15 ;
int z;
z=x;
```

The default value is 0 for the int type. When you assign a value of x to z, the value 15 is copied, which means one more value is added to the stack.

Reference types keep a reference or address on the stack, but allocate the real memory on the heap.

```
Obj redObj = new Obj("red");
Obj blueObj = new Obj("blue");
Obj someObj;
someObj = blueObj;
```

redObj = blueObj;

For example, as shown in the figure, when we create an object called redObj, the memory address allocated to the actual object is stored on the stack. The default value of the reference type is null, which means it does not hold any reference.

Assignment means copying the references. So when someObj is assigned with blueObj, a new object is not created in the memory heap for someObj. Instead a new reference to the existing object that is blueObj is added to the stack.

Again, if we assign the blueObj address to the redObj object reference as shown in figure 2, the redObj object reference is unused. Here the .NET Framework's smart garbage collection takes care of this.

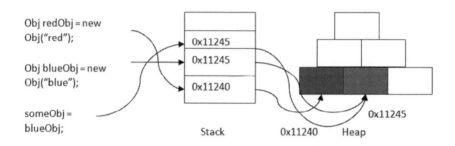

Fig 1: Example of reference type

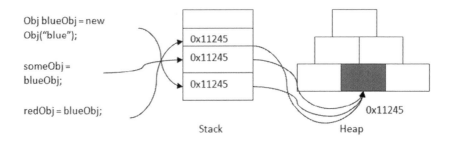

Obj blueObj = new
Obj("blue");

someObj =
blueObj;

redObj = blueObj;

0x11245

0x11245

0x11245

0x11245

Stack

Heap

Fig 2: Example of reference type

Boxing and Unboxing

Type Conversion is the conversion between data types. Before we proceed with type conversion, let us look at the need for it, by beginning to understand the various pre-defined types in C#. The common language specification defines the size for each type created. The byte type can hold one byte, the bool type can hold one byte, the char type can hold two bytes, the double type can hold eight bytes and the int type can hold four bytes.

Suppose we want to assign a value of a double variable to an int variable. This is not possible, as the size of the double data type is larger than that of integer data type. Hence we need type conversion.

Now that we have seen the necessity for type conversions, we will see how C# makes this possible. Type conversion comes in two flavors, namely the Implicit conversions and the Explicit conversions. Let us look at implicit conversions. When we declare a variable x as an integer and assign it a value of 3456789, four bytes of memory is allocated for the variable x. If we declare a variable y

34

as a long integer and assign it a value of x, eight bytes of memory are reserved for y and, since the size of y is more than that of x, it can easily accommodate the value of x within it. This is a typical example of implicit conversion.

Explicit conversions require a cast, an operator that explicitly converts an expression from one data type to a different data type. The general syntax of explicit conversion is as shown below:

float x = 20.5;
int y = int(x);

When we assign a double variable to an integer variable, an explicit cast is required. This may or may not succeed and the information might be lost. When we try to cast a character to a Boolean data type, the conversion will not be possible and it will result in a compile-time error as shown below:

char c = 's';
bool d = (bool) c ; //This gives compile time error.

In the order of widening conversion, if you assign a byte data type to short, it is an implicit conversion. If the order is reversed and you assign a short data type to byte, it is an explicit conversion that requires type casting as shown in the figure 3 and 4.

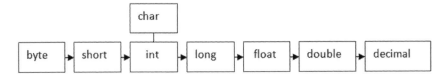

Fig 3: Implicit Conversion

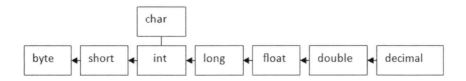

Fig 4: Explicit Conversion

Since C# supports the Unified Type System, it provides a special type of Implicit and Explicit Conversion called Boxing and Unboxing. As shown in figure 5, when an integer x is assigned a value of 20, its value is copied into the stack. First, an object reference o is created on the stack and when o is assigned the value x, the object reference is created on the stack; this points to the allocated object instance on the heap.

When you assign 20.986f to an object o, the value from the instance is copied into the value-type variable.

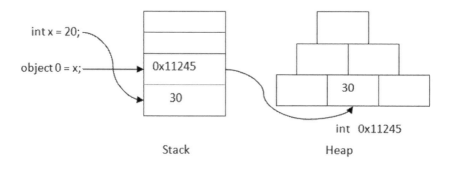

Fig 5: Boxing in C#

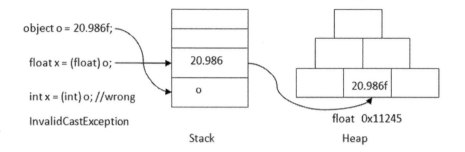

Fig 6: Unboxing in C#

Pre-Defined Value Types

Here is a list of pre-defined value types provided by C#.

- **Integer:** uint, long, sbyte, ushort, byte, int, ulong, short.

- **Floating Point:** float, decimal, double.

- **Character:** char.

- **Boolean:** bool.

CTS type	Alias Name
System.Int32	int
System.Char	char
System.Double	double

As we can see above, int is the alias name for the common type system or CTS int 32. That is the reason why we use int without using the using system directive.

Pre-Defined Reference Types

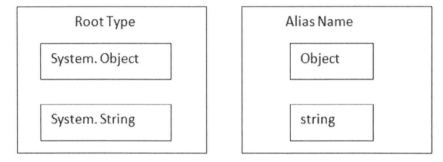

Fig 7: Pre-defined reference type in C#

The pre-defined reference types in C# are string and object. We will see strings in detail in the next section. Objects are discussed in the knowledge asset of the kshop titled "C# 2.0 – Simple C# Program and Namespace". Since C# provides a class called String Builder which is defined under the namespace System.Text, we will study strings by comparing the two. But before we proceed, we will see the difference between string with a capital s and string with a small s.

If you are using string with a small s, it is a language-specific alias to the underlying .NET Framework. So just like how you can use int, double and object without using the Using System directive, you can use string with a small s. However, if you use string with a capital S, you will have to use the Using System directive. So it is just the choice of the programmer.

Strings and StringBuilders

A string is a sequence of characters in a contiguous memory allocation. Whenever you create a string s1, an object reference s1 is created; this refers to a string, "good", created in a string intern pool managed by the .NET Framework as shown in figure 8.

string s1 = "good";

Similarly, the string "day" is created in the string intern pool.

string s2 = "day";

Suppose you call a method ToUpper, defined in the string class; since string is immutable, the string "good" in the pool does not change to capitals.

s1.ToUpper();

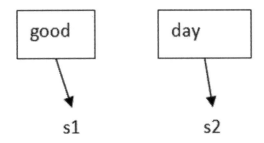

Fig 8: String intern pool - strings

When we overwrite the same to s1 again, then the pointer will point to "good" which is in capitals as shown in figure 9.

s1=s1.ToUpper();

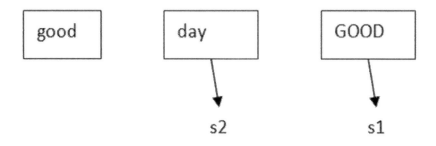

Fig 9: String intern pool - strings

If we create another string, s3, with "good", a reference to the already existing "good" in the pool is created as shown in figure 10.

string s3 = "good";

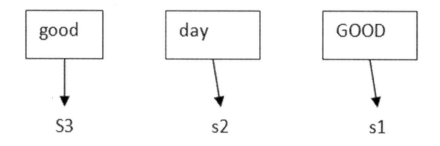

Fig 10: String intern pool - strings

The StringBuilder feature is unique to C#. Whenever you create a StringBuilder object which is defined under System.Text namespace s1, an object s1 is created and it refers to the string "good" created in the string intern pool managed by the .NET Framework. Similarly, the string "a" is created in the string intern pool as shown in figure 11.

Using System.Text;

StringBuilder s1 = new StringBuilder("good");

StringBuilder s2 = new StringBuilder("a");

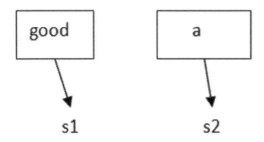

Fig 11: String intern pool - StringBuilder

The ToUpper method converts the value of the character to uppercase as shown in figure 12.

s2[0] = Char.ToUpper(s2[0]);

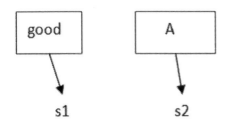

Fig 12: String intern pool - StringBuilder

You can print a StringBuilder object and, here, the ToString method is called implicitly.

Console.WriteLine(s2); //s2.ToString() is called implicitly

If we call the methods defined in StringBuilder like the Append function, you can see "hi" is appended to s1 as shown in figure 12. This is because StringBuilders are mutable.

s1.Append("hi");

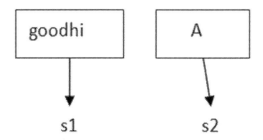

Fig 12: String intern pool - StringBuilder

Now if we perform the same operation using strings, we can see one more string is created unnecessarily as shown in figure 13.

s1 += "hi";

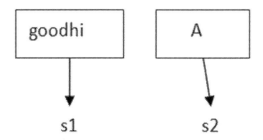

Fig 13: String intern pool - strings

So, it is a good practice to use the StringBuilder class rather than string when modification of string is involved as it saves memory. The Smart Garbage Collector of the .NET Framework takes care of the unused objects.

So let us summarize what we have learnt by comparing Strings and StringBuilder in the following Table (table1).

Strings	StringBuilders
➤ Strings are immutable.	➤ The StringBuilder object is mutable.
➤ It has read only properties like Length.	➤ It has read only properties like Length, Capacity and MaxCapacity.
➤ It also has methods like ToLower(), ToUpper() and Substring()	➤ It also has methods like Append(), Insert(), Remove(), Replace() which helps in modifying its contents.

Table 1: Comparison between Strings and StringBuilder

Strings are immutable. So, every time some modifications are done to the string, a new string object needs to be created. StringBuilder object is mutable; it can be used to modify an existing string and there is no need to create a fresh string. StringBuilder has read only properties, such as Length, Capacity and MaxCapacity. We will learn about read only properties in detail in the chapters that follow.

It also has methods like Append, Insert, Remove and Replace. Strings have read only properties like length. They also have methods like ToLower, ToUpper and Substring.

More about Strings

In the below statement, d is a string object.

    string d = "good day";

Normally, we use escape characters to store a string like the string s1 and the output in such cases will be similar to other programming languages.

    string s1 = "\\\\d\\sysroot\\filename.dll";
    // Output
    "\\d\sysroot\filename.dll"

There are some cases, however, where we may have to use strings that can span multiple lines or where white spaces need to be preserved, like the string s2 here.

    string s2 = @"\\d\sysroot\filename.dll";
    // Output
    "\\d\sysroot\filename.dll"

However, there might be a need to use double quotes within the verbatim string literal. In such a case, the above syntax will fail and we must use another double quote to escape it as follows.

string text = @"The word ""good"" contains four letters."
\\ Output
"The word "good" contains four letters."

Chapter 4

Methods in C#

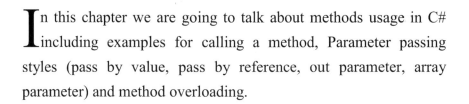

In this chapter we are going to talk about methods usage in C# including examples for calling a method, Parameter passing styles (pass by value, pass by reference, out parameter, array parameter) and method overloading.

C# Methods

"Method" is a code block which contains set of statements. Every method should be in a class or struct.

Declaration:

```
AccessModifier _Modifier ReturnType MethodName(Parameterlist)
{
Method body (set of statements)
}
```

AccessModifiers: is a keyword that decides nature of accessibility and mode of application of the method.

List of modifiers are:

Access Modifier		Description
C#	VB.NET	
Public	Public	Access from anywhere including outside the class
Private	Private	Access limited to within the class. This is the default one if we did not specify access modifier
Protected	Protected	Access limited to within the class and type that inherits from the class
Internal	Friend	Access limited to classes defined in the present assembly
Protected internal	Protected friend	Access is limited to the current assembly and types derived from the containing class.

_Modifier		Description
C#	VB.NET	
new		Hides inherited method within same signature
static		Not operated on instance of class

virtual		Method Can be overridden by child class
override		Overrides abstract or virtual method in derived class
Extern		Method is to implement external in some other language
Sealed		Cannot be overridden by any derived classes
abstract		Virtual method with signature and without implementation

Parameter list – list of parameters to function.

E.g.: public void Add(int a,int b,int c) – a,b,c are parameters to function

The common method which is used in every program is the **Main method**. This is an entry point to execute a program and should be static; its return type is int or void.

```
public static void Main()
public static int Main()
public static void Main(string[] args)
public static int Main(string[] args)
```

The parameter, args, will be a value which is provided from a command line argument.

Calling a Method

The process of activating a method is known as calling a method. This can be done like

yourClassObjectName.yourMethodName(parameters)

Example:

```
class CallingMethod
{
    public string HelloMethod()
    {
        return "Hello. I am from calling method";
    }
}
class CallingMethodUsage
{
    public static void Main()
    {
        string text = string.Empty;
        //Object creation to activate method
        CallingMethod obj = new CallingMethod();
        //calling method
        text=obj.HelloMethod();
        Console.WriteLine(text);
        //calling static method
        Console.WriteLine(HelloStaticMethod());
        Console.ReadLine();
    }
    public static string HelloStaticMethod()
    {
        return "Hello. I am from calling static method";
    }
}
```

Note: if your method is static then no need to create an object. You can directly call the static method like HelloStaticMethod.

Method Overloading

Definition: Method overloading is a concept of using the same method name with a differing number type and order of arguments.

When to use: If a method is performing a similar action but using different parameters then we can use method overloading.

Example: if we want to add two integers or two float values we can write methods like

Before method overlaoding		After method overloading

public int AddIntValues(int a1, int a2)
 	
{
 	
   return a1 + a2;
 	
}
public float AddFloatValues(float a1, float a2)
 	
{
 	
   return a1 + a2;
 	
}
	→	public int Add(int a1, int a2)
		
		{
		
		   return a1 + a2;
		
		}
		public float Add(float a1, float a2)
		
		{
		
		   return a1 + a2;
		
		}

The compiler will identify which method to execute based on number of arguments and their data types during compilation. This is an example of compile time polymorphism.

Example:

```
class Base
    {
        public int Add(int a1, int a2)
        {
            return a1 + a2;
        }
        public float Add(int a1, float a2)
        {
            return a1 + a2;
        }
    }
    class Derived : Base
    {
        public int Add(int a1, int a2, int a3)
        {
            return a1 + a2 + a3;
        }
        public float Add(float a1, int a2)
        {
            return a1 + a2;
        }
    }

    class MethodOverloadingUsage
    {
        static void Main()
        {
            Derived obj = new Derived();
            Console.WriteLine(obj.Add(10, 20));
            Console.WriteLine(obj.Add(10, 12.5f));
            Console.WriteLine(obj.Add(10, 20, 30));
```

```
        Console.WriteLine(obj.Add(13.5f, 10));
        Console.Read();
    }
}
```

Output:
30
22.5
60
23.5

Notes:

- Return type of method will not be considered for overloading usage

- Same method name provides different forms so it is example of polymorphism.

REF and OUT in C#

In C#, methods have a limitation in that they can't return more than a single value to a calling method or a calling point in a code piece.

```
public int Compute(int a, int b)
    {
        a = a * 10;
        b = a + b;
        return a;
    }
```

In this example, if we call this method, it would return only a single value at a time either a or b.

There could be some situations when we need more than one value to be returned from a method. Using the default parameter types passing behavior, we can't return more than one value from a method.

When arguments are passed to a method, conceptually the runtime generates a copy and passes that copy to the method. It is actually a copy of the passed variable that is available inside the method. If the value got changed inside the method, the actual value will not be changed outside the method.

```
class Program
    {
    static void Main(string[] args)
        {

        int iNum = 10;
        Increment(iNum);
        Console.Write("value of a is:" + iNum);
        Console.Read();

        }
    public static void Increment(int b)
        {
        b = b + 10;
        }
    }
```

Output

```
value of a is:10
```

Because copy of the variable iNum is passed to method Increment (), not the variable iNum.

So the changes made to iNum would not be reflected outside Increment ().

C# provides "**ref**" & "**out**" parameter keywords to overcome with this. By using these keywords, the behavior of passed variables could be changed easily. These keywords also known as **Method Parameter Keywords**.

REF keyword

By default, method parameters are passed by value behavior. By using "ref" keyword, the parameter's behavior will be changed. When "ref" is used with the parameter, that will be passed by reference behavior. Hence, the changes made to the parameter in the called method will be reflected back to the calling environment i.e. the calling method.

By using "ref", multiple values can be return from a single method.

For implementing the "ref" parameter, both the method definition/signature and the calling method ref must be explicitly specified with the passed parameters.

The variable must be initialized before passing the "ref" parameter to a method, i.e. the value must be assigned to the variable before passing it to method.

Out keyword

The "Out" key word is similar to the ref keyword. It also allows parameters to pass by reference to a method. This is used for passing variables for output purposes in most cases.

By using "out", we can also return multiple values from a single method.

Like "ref", "out" must be explicitly specified with the passed parameters in both the method definition/signature and the calling method, while implementing the parameter.

Variable initialization is not necessary before passing the "out" parameter to a method. But the variable must be initialized before returning to the calling environment (calling method) i.e. the value must be assigned to the variable.

Example: -

```
using System;
using System.Collections.Generic;
using System.Text;

namespace ConsoleApplication1
{
    class Program
```

```
{
    static void Main(string[] args)
    {
        int rectArea = 0;
        int perimeter = 0;
        double area;
        double circumfrence;
        Console.Write("\n****Without using Ref/Out paramter Types****");
        Calculate(10, 5, rectArea, perimeter);
        Console.Write("\nvalue of rectArea is:" + rectArea);
        Console.Write("\nvalue of perimeter is:" + perimeter);
        Calculate(5, 5, rectArea, perimeter);
        Console.Write("\nvalue of rectArea is:" + rectArea);
        Console.Write("\nvalue of perimeter is:" + perimeter);
        Console.Write("\n\n******* Ref Keyword Example *********");
        Compute(10, 5, ref rectArea, ref perimeter);
        Console.Write("\nvalue of rectArea is:" + rectArea);
        Console.Write("\nvalue of perimeter is:" + perimeter);
        Compute(5, 5, ref rectArea, ref perimeter);
        Console.Write("\nvalue of rectArea is:" + rectArea);
        Console.Write("\nvalue of perimeter is:" + perimeter);
        AreaForCircle(10, out area, out circumfrence);
        Console.Write("\nvalue of area is:" + area);
        Console.Write("\nvalue of circumfrence is:" + circumfrence);
        Console.Read();
    }
        public static void Calculate(int side, int side1, int rectArea, int perimeter)
```

```csharp
    {
        if (side == side1)
        {
            Console.Write("\n\n****** FOR SQUARE ********");
            rectArea = side * side;
            perimeter = 4 * side;
        }
        else
        {
            Console.Write("\n\n******       FOR       RECTANGLE ********");
            rectArea = side * side1;
            perimeter = 2 * (side + side1);
        }
    }

    public static void Compute(int side, int side1, ref int rectArea, ref int perimeter)
    {
        if (side == side1)
        {
            Console.Write("\n\n****** FOR SQUARE ********");
            rectArea = side * side;
            perimeter = 4 * side;
        }
        else
        {
            Console.Write("\n\n******       FOR       RECTANGLE ********");
            rectArea = side * side1;
            perimeter = 2 * (side + side1);
```

```
            }
        }

        public static void AreaForCircle(int radius, out double area,
out double circumfrence)
        {
            Console.Write("\n\n******* OUT Keyword Example
*********");
            area = 3.14 * radius * radius;
            circumfrence = 2 * radius * 3.14;
        }
    }
}
```

Output

Note:

Parameters with "ref" and "out" are similar at compile time i.e. they behave almost the same.

Method overloading can't be allowed if the only difference is the ref and out parameter type between the methods definition. It will result in compile time error.

Chapter 5

Method Overloading Vs Overriding in C#

Polymorphism is an important concept of Object Oriented Programming (OOPs). Polymorphism means having different forms. It can also be defined as 'One Interface, multiple functions.' It means that a variable or a method can be used in more than one form. Polymorphism helps in reducing the effort of writing the entire code by reusing the existing methods.

There are 2 types of Polymorphism: Static polymorphism and Dynamic polymorphism.

Static Polymorphism

In this type of polymorphism, the compiler knows which of the methods has to be called at compile time itself, since each method will have a different signature. Method overloading is an example of Static Polymorphism.

There are 2 ways in using Static Polymorphism.

1. Method Overloading

2. Operator Overloading

Method Overloading

Method overloading is the process of creating more than one method having the same name, but different signatures. Creating a method in the child class with the same name as in the parent class is Method Overloading. One important point to be noted while creating overloaded methods is that the data types and/or number of arguments of the methods should be different.

Example 1 [Invalid Example]: The following example will throw an error, since both the methods in the class 'First' have the same return type (int), the same name (sum) and the same argument type and number. Hence the below example **is not method overloading**.

```
using System;
namespace overloading
{
        class First
        {
                public int sum(int val1)
                {
                        return val1+1;
                }

                public int sum(int val2)
```

```
            {
                        return val2+1;
            }
    }
    class mainClass
    {
        public static void main()
      {
        First fObj = new First();
        fObj.sum(2);
      }
    }

}
```

Output:

Example 2 [Invalid Example]: The following example shows two methods having different return types, but the same method name, and signature. On execution, this will throw a compile time error, since the compiler will not know which method is being called.

```
using System;
namespace overloading
{
        class First
        {
                public int sum(int val1)
                {
                        return val1+1;
                }

        public void sum(int val2)
        {
                        Console.Write(val2+1);
        }
        }
    class mainClass
        {
        public static void main()
        {
                First fObj = new First();
                int a=fObj.sum(2);
        }
        }
}
```

Output:

Example 3 [Valid Example]: The following example will not throw any error and is a valid example of method overloading. The methods in the class 'First' have the same name (Sum), but different signatures.

```
using System;
namespace overloading
{
class First
    {
    public int sum(int val1)  //This method has one argument, while
the next method has two. Hence during compilation, system will
identify it as 2 different methods.
        {
```

```
                        return val1 + 1;
    }

    public int sum(int val1, int val2)
    {
                        return val2 + val2;
    }
}

class Program
{
    static void Main(string[] args)
    {
        First fobj = new First();
        int val = fobj.sum(3);
        Console.WriteLine("sum= " + val);
    }
}
}
```

Output:

Example 4 [Valid Example]: A simple program demonstrating Method Overloading. The following program performs addition of numbers. The same method 'sum()' is used for this purpose. The compiler decides which method to call based on the method call.

```
using System;
using System.Collections.Generic;
using System.Linq;
using System.Text;

namespace overloading
{

    public class First
    {
        public int sum(int val1)
        {
                    return val1 + 1;
        }

        public int sum(int val1, int val2)
        {
                    return val1 + val2;
        }
        public float sum(float val1, float val2, float val3)
        {
                    return val1 + val2 + val3;
        }
    }
    class second
    {
            public static void Main()
        {
```

```
        int value1, value2;
    float value3;
        First obj1 = new First();
    value1 = obj1.sum(100);
    Console.WriteLine("Sum Of Integer + 1 = " + value1);
    value2 = obj1.sum(10, 20);
    Console.WriteLine("Sum Of Two Integers = " + value2);
    value3 = obj1.sum(1.5f, 1.5f, 1.5f);
    Console.WriteLine("Sum of three floating point numbers = "+
value3);
        }
    }

}
```

Explanation of the Program:

1) Execution starts from the Main() method.

2) The object 'obj1' of class 'First' is created.

3) The object 'obj1' is used to call the 'sum() method. 1 argument of 'int' type is passed to the function. The method call matches to the following method definition:

    public int sum(int val1)

Hence, the compiler makes a call to this method. The result is stored in the variable 'value1' and will be printed as "Sum Of Integer + 1 = value1".

4) Object 'obj1' calls 'sum()' method with two integer arguments. The following method definition matches to the call:

   public int sum(int val1, int val2)

   This method is called and the result is stored in the variable 'value2' and will be printed as "Sum Of Two Integers = value2"

5) In the next line, the object 'obj' calls 'sum()' with three floating point arguments. Hence, the following method gets called:

   public float sum(float val1, float val2, float val3)

The result from this method is stored in the variable 'value3' and will be printed as "Sum of three floating point numbers = value3"

Output:

```
C:\Windows\system32\cmd.exe
Sum Of Integer + 1 = 101
Sum Of Two Integers = 30
Sum of three floating point numbers = 4.5
Press any key to continue . . .
```

Operator Overloading

Operator overloading is an example of Static Polymorphism. It provides a way to define and use operators such as +, -, *, and / for user-defined classes. It consists of a method declared by the keyword, 'operator', followed by an operator. This special method named operator is mainly used to perform overloading in C#.

Syntax for overloading:

```
return-data-type operator symbol-of-operator (arguments)
{
// define the function here
}
```

Dynamic Polymorphism

Dynamic Polymorphism is the process of deciding which method will be executed at run time. It provides a high level of data abstraction since it is done at run time. It is an important concept of Object Oriented Programming.

Method Overriding

This is the concept whereby a child class modifies the behavior inherited by it from the parent class. The methods that get inherited from the parent class can be modified by the child class. This is useful in situations where the child class needs to make use of the parent class functionality, but with some modifications.

It helps in the concept of 'Program Re-use', and hence saves effort. Method overriding can be achieved only if both the parent class method and the child class method have the same name, argument list, and return type. If there is any difference, then it is not considered overriding.

Example 1[Valid example]: The following example demonstrates the working of Method Overriding. The program calculates the area of a shape. The shape is decided at run-time based on the object created. One method called 'Area' is declared in the parent class 'Shape'. Two child classes (square and rectangle) inherit from the parent class (Shape). These child classes contain methods which override the 'Area' method in the parent class.

```
using System;
using System.Collections.Generic;
using System.Linq;
using System.Text;

namespace polymorp
{

    public class shape       //Base class
    {
        protected int length, breadth;
        public shape(int L = 0, int B = 0)
        {
            length = L;
            breadth = B;
        }
        public virtual void area()       // method to be overridden
```

```csharp
        {
            Console.WriteLine("Parent method");
        }

}
public class square : shape     //Child class
    {
        public square(int L = 0, int B = 0)
            : base(L, B)

        { }
        public override void area()
        {
            Console.WriteLine("Area of square= " + (length * breadth));
        }
}

    public class rectangle : shape     //Child class
    {
        public rectangle(int L = 0, int B = 0)
            : base(L, B)
        { }
        public override void area()
        {
            Console.WriteLine("Area  of  rectangle= " + (2 * (length +
breadth)));
        }

}

    public class callerClass
    {
        public void callShape(shape sObj)
```

```
        {
            sObj.area();
        }
    }
    class Program
    {
        static void Main(string[] args)
        {
            callerClass cObj = new callerClass();
            square sObj = new square(2, 3);
            cObj.callShape(sObj);
            rectangle rObj = new rectangle(2, 3);
            cObj.callShape(rObj);
        }
    }
}
```

Output:

```
C:\Windows\system32\cmd.exe
Area of square= 6
Area of rectangle= 10
Press any key to continue . . .
```

Virtual keyword:

For a method in the parent class to be overridden, it should be prefixed with the keyword, 'Virtual'.

Syntax:

<<access modifier>> virtual <<return type>> <<method name>> <<argument list with type>>;

Override keyword:

This keyword allows new changes to be made to the method of the parent class. For this keyword to be used, the base class method and the child class method should have the same signature.

Syntax:

<<access modifier>> override <<return type>> <<method name>> <<argument list with type>>; Differences between Method Overloading and Method Overriding:

Difference between Method Overloading and Method Overriding

Some of the main points of difference between method overloading and method overriding are given below:

Method Overloading	Method Overriding
The overloaded methods have different signatures, i.e. the number and / or types of arguments should be different	The methods involved have the same name, return type and signature
No keyword has to be used explicitly for overloading	virtual and override keywords are used for method overriding
It is an example of static polymorphism. The compiler knows which method is being called at the compile time itself.	It is an example of dynamic polymorphism. The method to be called is determined at run time. The compiler will not know at compile time.
More than one method can be created in a class with same name and with multiple arguments	Method created in Base class will be used in derived class with same set of arguments

Chapter 6

Loops in C#

A loop is used in C# - and many other programming languages – for repeated instructions. The basic functionality of the loop revolves around repeating a particular set of instructions or statements. Various loops have diverse conditions that stop them.

Naturally, if there are any statements or commands after the loop, the program progresses. Otherwise, the program ends.

There are three loops used in C#

1. For

2. While

3. Do While.

They have some fundamental differences in methodology. However, the end purpose is the same: repeating statements.

Structure of for Loop

The "for" loop focuses on repetitive execution of a certain set of instructions. This repetition continues until a pre-described condition returns a false value.

In the "for" loop, there are three components:

1. Initialization: In this step, the developer declares a variable. Along with the declaration, it is necessary to set an initial value for the variable too. This variable is to be used in the other two parts of "for" loop.

2. Conditional Expression: A pre-defined condition in Boolean form. Being Boolean means that the condition shall return either a "true" or "false" value. If the value returned is "false," the loop ends. An example of conditional expression can be variable < 10, where the loop continues until the variable reaches 10.

3. Steps: These steps are the increment or decrement in the loop variable value — for example, an increase or decrease of 1 in the value of the variable, etc.

After defining the components of the loop, the developer defines the instructions that are to be carried out.

Example of for Loop

The below example considers using the for loop for multiple iterations of a variable until a specific value is reached.

75

The first line is

for (int b = 0; b < 15; b++)

Here, we first declared the variable "b" and initialized its value to be "0". Secondly, we also mentioned the conditional expression. Here, we have determined that, if the value of b remains lower than 15, the loop shall continue. However, once the value of "b" goes to 15, the loop shall stop. Finally, we mentioned the step for the increment. Here, each loop will increment the value of b by 1. This process shall continue until "b" reaches 15, when the loop shall stop.

After this part, we shall write the instructions for the commands that are to be repeated. Let us use a simple output command to demonstrate the process. The next line shall be

```
{
        Console.WriteLine( "b current value: {0}", b);
}
```

This particular command shall display the value of b after the increment in each loop. As a result, the first output shall be "b current value: 0", while the last output shall be "b current value: 14". It is interesting to note that the value of the previous iteration shall not be displayed. The reason is that as soon as the value of "b" reaches 15, the loop shall stop, so the instruction to show the value shall not be executed.

Where to use for loop

It is preferable to use the for loop where the developer is particular about the number of iterations to be performed. For example, in our code, the number of iterations was 15. However, if the amount is not specified, the for loop may not be useful. In such cases, other loops are to be used.

Structure of While Loop

The while loop is preferred for repeating a set of instructions until a certain Boolean expression reaches a predefined level. Each iteration checks at the start to see if the condition mentioned is giving a true or a false value. If the value is still true, another iteration occurs. However, if the value becomes false, the iteration stops. Thus, in the while loop, the declaration of the variable and the initialization is made outside the loop. If the initialization is done inside the loop, it shall be repeated every time.

As a general structure:

1. Declare and Initialize the variable

2. While (Conditional Expression)

3. Set of Instructions

Example of While Loop

Let us use the same example from the "for" loop. It can be adapted to the while loop as follows int b = 0;

In this statement, we have successfully declared the variable and initialized its value to be 0. Now we can apply the loop

```
while (b < 15)
```

This statement starts the loop. It contains the conditional expression that the loop shall continue until the value of b is less than 15. Once the value reaches 15, the loop shall stop. Again, interestingly, this condition shall be checked at the start of each loop.

```
{
    Console.WriteLine( "b current value: {0}", b);
    b++;
}
```

In the given scenario, first the value of b shall be displayed, then the value shall be incremented by 1 in each loop. As a result, the first value shall be 0, while the last value shall be 14. However, if the placement of the instructions is changed, then the output can differ. To understand this, consider what will happen on the 14th iteration. First, the value shall be output as 14. Then, there shall be an iteration which will increase the value to 15. However, before this value can be displayed in the next iteration, the loop will end because the conditional expression shall give a false value. On the other hand, if the expression is changed a bit to:

```
{
b++;
    Console.WriteLine( "b current value: {0}", b);
}
```

Here, the first value shall be 1 because, before displaying the first value, there shall already be an increase in the value. As a result, the last value in this expression shall be 15, because the value will increment before being displayed.

Where to use While loop

The while loop is best used in situations where a certain number of iterations have to be conducted, but the increment or decrement has to be done inside the loop.

Structure of Do While Loop

The significant difference between the do-while loop and the while loop is that in the do-while loop, the set of instructions shall be performed at least once. The reason is that this loop tests the conditional statement at the end of each iteration. Thus, if you are using the while loop in the above example, and the initial value of b is 15 or above, the instructions in the loop shall not even process once. However, in the do-while loop the process shall occur once at least. Take a look at the structure to understand why:

1. Initialization and Declaration

2. Do (to start the loop

3. Instructions

4. While (Conditional Expression)

Thus, the loop condition is tested at the end of each iteration.

Example of Do-While Loop

We shall re-produce the same example in the do-while loop.

```
int b = 0;
```

We declared the variable b and initialized the value to be 0.

```
do
{
    Console.WriteLine( "b current value: {0}", b);
b++;
}  while (b < 15)
```

It is interesting to note here that, in the do-while loop, the setting of the instructions still matters. The above-given expression shall produce the values from "b current value: 0" to "b current value: 14". Before the 15th value can be displayed, the loop shall end. Just like the while loop, changing the setting of the instructions shall allow for a different output.

```
{
b++;
    Console.WriteLine( "b current value: {0}", b);
}
```

Here, the outputs shall be from "b current value: 1" to "b current value: 15", as the increment occurs before the display of the value.

Where to use Do while Loop

The Do While loop is used best where at least one iteration of the loop is necessary. The loop ensures that the set of instructions are performed at least once before the loop ends.

Loops of other Kinds

Apart from the basic loops – i.e., single loops – loops can be used inside loops. This approach is called using nested loops. Here, one loop is performing its function inside another loop. Practically, there can be an infinite number of loops performing within a single loop. It depends on the uses and the functionality required when deciding if nested loops are to be used. At the same time, any of the three types of loops can be used within another loop. There is no restriction on using the same kinds of loops.

Another loop that can be used is the infinite loop. Such a loop can be easily made with the for loop structure. Here, there is an infinite number of iterations as there is no conditional expression to stop the loop.

Generally, loops can be controlled by any numeric data type. These types can include double (digit) numbers or decimals etc.

Therefore, Loops are an important utility in C# to make development easier and more effective. Some basic functions cannot be performed without using loops. Generally, it takes some time to master the use of loops in C#. However, once a person can use them dexterously, they can be a powerful tool for significant development of quality programs.

Chapter 7

Collections in C#

Whenever it comes to storing data in a structured format, the best solution that programmers think of is arrays. However, though arrays are the best data structures available, they have the limitation of fixed size. Once an array is declared, it cannot accommodate data beyond its size. Hence the need for collection arises. Data can be pushed and popped into a collection as and when needed without worrying about its size.

Introduction

Collections are data structures in C#. They allow creation and modification of a group of objects. Memory management is handled automatically and the capacity of the collection can be expanded as required. Hence it is possible to add objects in a collection whenever needed.

The .NET framework supports three types of collections: -

- **General purpose:** - These collections implement basic data structures like dynamic arrays, stacks and queues. They include dictionaries in which key/value pairs can be stored. They hold elements of the type "**Object**" which is the base class for all types. Hence these collections are capable of holding any type of data.

- **Specialized:** - They operate on specific type of data or operate in a unique way. For instance, there are specialized collections for strings.

- **Bit based:** - Those collections store groups of bits. They support different sets of operations than other collections which are meant to operate only on the bits. For example, "BitArray" which is the main bit-based collection, supports bitwise operations like AND, OR and XOR.

The concept of "**enumerator**" is fundamental to every collection, which is supported by IEnumerable and Ienumerator interfaces. An enumerator provides a standard way of accessing elements within a collection. Since every collection must implement IEnumerable, the developers have the advantage of using the methods of Ienumerator to access the contents of a collection.

Collection classes and interfaces are available in the namespace **System.Collections**. All the collection classes are designed around the collection interfaces.

The different types of collection interface available are: -

- **Icollection:** -It is the foundation for all the collection classes.

- **Ilist:** - It inherits Icollection and defines the behavior of a collection with zero based indexes.

- **Idictionary:** - It defines the behavior of a collection that maps unique keys to values.

- **IEnumerable:** - This interface should be implemented by a class which wants to support enumerators.

- **Ienumerator:** - It defines the functionality of an enumerator and is used to cycle through the contents of a collection.

- **IdictionaryEnumerator:** - It can be called as an extension of Ienumerator and facilitates the enumeration of dictionaries.

- **Icomparable:** - It is used to compare collections.

The different type of built in collection classes available are: -

- **Stack:** - It is a first-in, last-out list.

- **Queue:** - It a first-in, first-out list.

- **HashTable:** - It stores key/value pairs.

- **BitArray:** - It is a collection of bits.

- **ArrayList:** - It is a dynamic array.

- **SortedList:** - It is a sorted list of key/value pairs.

- **HashSet:** - It is an unordered collection containing unique elements.

- **Dictionary:** It is collection of keys and values stored in an object called dict.

Let's see in detail the collection classes available in C#. It does not elaborate on collection interfaces.

Types of Collection Classes

Stacks

Stack is a data structure in which objects are arranged in Last In First Out (LIFO) manner. The element that is added at the end is the one that comes out first. Usually elements are inserted and removed from one end called the "top".

Queues

Queue is a data structure in which objects are arranged in a First In First Out (FIFO) manner. Here the elements at added at the rear end and removed from the front end.

Hash Tables

Hash table is a collection of key/value pairs that maps a key to a value. These pairs are arranged based on the hash code of the key. The keys are used as indexes to retrieve the corresponding values. There cannot be duplicate keys in a hash table. Both keys and values are of Object datatype.

Array Lists

Array List is similar to an array with the exception that its size can be dynamically increased or decreased as and when required. Also elements can be inserted at any position in the array list unlike arrays. It's a kind of an array where objects can be added even after instantiation.

Sorted Lists

A Sorted List is a collection of key/value pairs similar to a Hash Table but here the list is sorted on the basis of the keys. The elements are accessible both by keys and indexes. Thus a Sorted List resembles a Hash Table enriched with functions of an array.

Bit Arrays

Bit Arrays are arrays of bit values which have either a true or false Boolean value. A true value means the bit is on (1) and false value means the bit is off (0).

The BitArray is the best class which can be easily used to perform bitwise operations and to display the bits.

HashSet

HashSet was introduced in the .NET Framework 3.5, and it's an unordered collection which has unique elements in it. It contains all the basic operation methods like Contains, Add, and Remove. HashSet is used in implementing Icollection.

These are some of the properties and advantages of HashSet:

1. It is modeled after a math set, and the elements in it should be unique.

2. HashSet is designed to allow fast searches and make insertion faster.

3. Unlike dictionaries, they don't have indices to find the values but the operations are faster compared to a list

4. HashSet<T> could be used to get the duplicate values in a list of objects using a property of the object.

5. It preserves the added order of the objects at the cost of slower running times.

6. Since they don't use indices, accessing the elements could be done with the help of an enumerator.

Remove duplicate object from a list of objects using a property of the class.

Consider a class employee in the below example, it has Employee ID and Employee Name as Properties,

```
class Employee
{
    public long EmployeeID
    {
        get;
        set;
    }

    public string EmployeeName
    {
        get;
        set;
    }
}
```

Creating a list of Employee Object and adding employee objects to it

```
List<Employee> employeeList = new List<Employee>();

    Employee employee1 = new Employee();
    employee1.EmployeeID = 1001;
    employee1.EmployeeName = "ABC";

    Employee employee2 = new Employee();
    employee2.EmployeeID = 1002;
    employee2.EmployeeName = "DEF";
```

```
Employee employee3 = new Employee();
employee3.EmployeeID = 1001;
employee3.EmployeeName = "GHI";

employeeList.Add(employee1);
employeeList.Add(employee2);
employeeList.Add(employee3);
```

The employee list has two objects with the same Employee ID 1001. We could remove the duplicate objects by using HashSet, which is faster than the list operations.

We could have a static method to convert IEnumerable to Hashset.

```
public static class Extensions
    {
        public static HashSet<T> ToHashSet<T>(this IEnumerable<T> source)
        {
            return new HashSet<T>(source);
        }
    }
```

To fetch the objects where Employee ID is duplicate:
```
var duplicates = employeeList.GroupBy(i => new { i.EmployeeID })
        .Where(g => g.Count() > 1)
        .Select(g => g.Key);
var duplicateRecordset = Extensions.ToHashSet(duplicates);
List<Employee> duplicated = employeeList.FindAll(p =>
duplicateRecordset.Contains(new { p.EmployeeID}));
```

To fetch the objects where Combination of Employee ID and Employee Name is duplicate:

```
var duplicates = employeeList.GroupBy(i => new {
i.EmployeeID,i.EmployeeName})
        .Where(g => g.Count() > 1)
          .Select(g => g.Key);
 var duplicateRecordset = Extensions.ToHashSet(duplicates);
List<Employee> duplicated = employeeList.FindAll(p =>
duplicateRecordset.Contains(new {
p.EmployeeID,p.EmployeeName}));
```

The above is used when the combination of two properties in a class is duplicated.

In real time we could find the duplicates in a list which has thousands of records in a very short time.

Dictionary

Compare two lists and find the mismatched elements using dictionary in C#

The dictionary could be used to compare two lists having different objects with a common property amongst them.

Consider the below example,

```
class Employee
{
    public long EmployeeID
    {
        get;
```

```csharp
        set;
    }

    public string EmployeeName
    {
        get;
        set;
    }
}

class Manager
{
    public long EmployeeID
    {
        get;
        set;
    }

    public long ManagerID
    {
        get;
        set;
    }
}
```

Both the classes have a common property, EmployeeID, and dictionary could be used to compare two lists and select the items that mismatch.

```csharp
List<Employee> employeeList = new List<Employee>();
Employee employee1 = new Employee();
employee1.EmployeeID = 1001;
employee1.EmployeeName = "ABC";
```

```
Employee employee2 = new Employee();
employee2.EmployeeID = 1002;
employee2.EmployeeName = "DEF";

employeeList.Add(employee1);
employeeList.Add(employee2);
```

In the manager list, we have the manager2 object which has am Employee ID=1004; this is not present in the Employee list so we could use dictionary to find the mismatched Employee IDs.

```
List<Manager> employeeList = new List<Manager>();

Manager manager1 = new Manager();
manager1.EmployeeID = 1001;
manager1.ManagerID = 5001;

Manager manager2 = new Manager();
manager2.EmployeeID = 1004;
manager2.ManagerID = 5002;

managerList.Add(manager1);
managerList.Add(manager2);

long employeeCounter = 0;
long managerCounter = 0;
```

Creating a dictionary for employee and manager

```
Dictionary<long,long> employeeDictionary = new
Dictionary<long,long>();
Dictionary<long,long> managerDictionary = new
Dictionary<long,long>();

managerList.ForEach(delegate(Manager manager)
{
   managerCounter ++;
   if
(!employeeDictionary.ContainsKey(manager.EmployeeID))
      employeeDictionary.Add(manager.EmployeeID,
managerCounter);
});
```

```
List<long> MismatchedEmployeeIDs =
employeeDictionary.Keys.Except(managerDictionary.Keys).ToList();
```

Mismatched employee IDs list will hold the IDs which are present in the employee object and not in Manager Object and the same is true of the other way around. In real time, lists with millions of records could be compared in a few seconds, because dictionary is very much faster than list operations.

Basic Differences between Hashset and Dictionary

- Hashset allows multiple reader threads, but dictionary offers no thread safety.

- Value types in dictionary don't need boxing, but boxing is needed in Hashset.

- When we add multiple values to a dictionary, the order in which the items are added is maintained, but it's not maintained in Hashset.

- Dictionary is strongly typed, Hashset is weakly typed.

- Indexers can't be used in Hashset to access the items in it, whereas dictionary uses Indexers to access the items.

Hashset and dictionary generally perform better than list, however based on our requirements we need decide which one to use. List can be used if we need to just keep track of the items, Dictionary could be used if we need to hash lookup against some value, and Hashset can be used if we need to perform set operations.

Chapter 8

Generics in C#

G enerics is one of the new features introduced in C# 2.0. It introduces the concept of type parameters by which one can design generalized classes and methods. The types for these classes and methods will be finalized or specified at the time of instantiation. Generics allow us to create type safe classes and methods without actually committing to a data type.

Advantage of using Generics

- No Need of Casting
- Reduce the amount of Boxing and unboxing.
- Improve Type Safety.
- Create generalized types.
- Better Performance.
- Binary Code Reuse.
- Avoid Code Bloating.

Applying Generics

1. Custom Generic Classes

2. Generic Constraints

3. Inheritance in Generic

4. Generic Methods

5. Generic Delegate

6. Generic Interfaces

7. Iterators in Generics

Creating Custom Generic Classes

A Simple Generic Class

```
Class  ClassName <T>
{
........................
}
```

Here 'T' is a generic Type. It will be replaced by the real type when the object of the class is created.

Example:

```
using System;
using System.Collections.Generic;
using System.Linq;
using System.Text;
namespace SimpleGenericClass
{
    public class GenericClass<T> // T is a genereic Type
    {
```

```
    T var1; // Creating member variable of Genereic Type
    public  GenericClass(T  value1)  //  Constructor  Paramerter  as
       Generic Type
    {
       var1 = value1;
    }
    public T Get() // return type as Generic Parameter
    {
         return var1;
    }
    public void showDataType()
    {
       Console.WriteLine(" Type of T is " + typeof(T));
    }
  }
  class Program
  {
    static void Main(string[] args)
    {
       GenericClass<int>  obj1  =  new  GenericClass<int>(20);    //
       defining the type for T as int
       obj1.showDataType();
       int result = obj1.Get();
       Console.WriteLine(result);
GenericClass<string> obj2 ;
Obj2 = new GenericClass<string>("Office");); // defining the type for
       T as string;
       obj2.showDataType();
       string strresult = obj2.Get();
       Console.WriteLine(strresult);
    }
  }
}
```

Output:

Type of T is System.Int32

20

Type of T is System.String

Office

A Generic Class with Multiple Types

A Generic class can have multiple generic types as below:

```
Class ClassName <T, K>
{
…………………………………..
}
```

Example:

```
using System;
using System.Collections.Generic;
using System.Linq;
using System.Text;

namespace SimpleGenericClassDemo
{
    public class GenericClass<T,K> // T and K are parameter type.
    {
        T var1;
        K var2;
        public GenericClass( T value1, K value2)
        {
            var1 = value1;
```

```
        var2 = value2;
    }
    public void showDataType()
    {
        Console.WriteLine(" DataType of T: " + typeof(T));
        Console.WriteLine(" DataType of k: " + typeof(K));
    }
}

class MyMainClass
{
    public static void Main(String[] args)
    {
        GenericClass<int, float> obj1 = new GenericClass<int,
        float>(10,1.5F);
        obj1.showDataType(); // T replaced by int and k replaced
        by float
        GenericClass<string, int> obj2 = new GenericClass<string,
        int>("Pink", 22);
        obj2.showDataType();  // T replaced by string and k
        replaced by int
    }
}
```

The 'Default' Keyword

In Generic class constructors, if we want to initialize the generic type data members to the default value, it will be not possible because at the time the class is written, the data types are generic and the default value varies for every data type. In order to assign default values to generic type data members, the 'default' keyword is used. While instantiating the class, the default keyword will look at the real data type and assign the corresponding data types default value.

For example:

If we have class as follows:

```
Class MyClass<T, K>
{
    T  value1;
    K value2:
Public MyClass()
    {
            Value1= default(T);
            Value2 = default(K);

    }
}
```

Now, when I create the object of the class as below:

MyClass obj <int, string> = new MyClass<int, string>();

Value1 will be assigned 0 and value2 will be assigned 'null';

The default values are as below:

- Numerical values have a default value of **0.**

- Reference types have a default value of **null.**

- Fields of structures are set accordingly to 0 or **null.**

Generic Constraints

When we use a generalized type parameter, the generalized type is unbound and not constrained in any way. If a class is declared as generic as below:

Class MyClass<T> {}

Here, T is unbound. It can take any type while instantiating the object of the class. The C# compiler will convert the source code to IL code, independent of any argument type that the client will use. Because of this, there will be a lack of type safety. The generic code generated will be able to use methods, properties, or members of the generic type parameter which are incompatible with the specific type the client uses.

When we apply restriction to the type argument, and if a client code wants to have an instance of a generic class with the help of a type which isn't permitted by the constraint, it results in an error.

Types of Constraint

- Derivation Constraint

- Default Constructor Constraint

- Reference/Value type constraint

Constrain Type	Constraint	Description
Reference type constraint	Class myclass<T> Where T:class	Type T should be a reference (class) type.Ex *myclass<student> obj = new myclass<student>();* here student is a reference /class type.
Value type constraint	Class myclass<T> where T:struct	Type T should be a value type. Ex: *myclass<int> obj = new myclass<int>();*
Default Constructor constraint	Class myclass<T> where T:new()	Type T should have a parameterless constructor. Ex *Myclass <student> obj = new myclass<student>();* here student class should have a parameterless constructor.
Derivation constraint	Class myclass<T> where T: <base class name>	Type T should be of the type base class or its derived class. Ex : *class Person{}* *Class Student:Person{}* *Mclass<student> obj = new myclass<Student>();* Here Type T can take Person or Student only.
Derivation Constraint	Class myclass<T> where T:< Interface Name>	Type T should be of the type which had been implemented the interface. Type T can take only those classes which had been implemented the interface.

Generic Methods

A Generic Method is defined as below

```
Public class MyClass
{
Public void SwapElement<T>(ref T Element1 , ref T Element2)
{
T TempElement;
TempElement = Element1;
Element1 = Element2;
Element2 = TempElement;
    }
}
```

The following code shows how to call the method:

```
Public void TestMethod()
{
    int a = 10;
    int b = 20;
    String s1 = "day";
    String s2 = "night";
SwapElement(s1, s2);
SwapElement(a, b);
    }
```

Within a generic class, there can be two types of methods - generic and non–generic. Ex:

```
Public class MyClass<T>
{
    Public GenericMethod<X>( X n1 , Xn2) {}
    Public Non-GenericMethod( T n1 , T n2) {}
}
```

If we define a generic method with the same parameter type as the generic class, then it throws an error:

```
class GenericClass<T>
{
    // CS0693 error
    void Method<T> () { }
}
```

Reason for warning: within the method scope the inner T hides the argument supplied for the outer T. If we want to call a generic method inside a generic class, it has to be as below:

```
class GenericClass<T>
{
    //No warning
    void Method<U> () { }
}
```

A Generic Method can have constraint. A generic method can be overloaded like normal methods.

Generic Interface

Generic Interfaces are created as below

```
Interface IMyGenInterface<T>
```

```
    {
        T Method(T n1);
    }
```

A generic class can implement a generic interface as shown below:

```
    Class MyGenClass<T> : IMyGenInterface<T>
    {
        Public void Method(T n1)
        {return n1};
    }
    class MainClass
    {
        static void Main()
        {
        MyGenClass<int> intObject = new MyGenClass<int>();
        MyGenClass<string> stringObject = new MyGenClass<string
    >();

        Console.WriteLine("{0}", intObject.getValue(5));
        Console.WriteLine("{0}", stringObject.getValue(" Paulin. "));
        }
    }
```

If a non-generic class has to implement a generic interface, we have to specify the type value as shown below:

```
    Class MyClass : IMyGenInterface < int >
    {
        Public void Method(int n1)
        {return n1};
    }
```

Generic Delegates

A generic delegate defines its own type parameters. Code that references the generic delegate can specify the value of the type parameter to create a closed constructed type. Example:

```
using System;

delegate T MyDel<T>(T v);
  class MyClass {
  static int Add(int x) {
    return x;
  }
   static string Echo(string str) {
   return str;
  }
  public static void Main() {
    MyDel<int> intDel = sum;
    Console.WriteLine(intDel(3));
    MyDel<string> strDel = Echo;
    Console.WriteLine(strDel(" Hello "));
  }
}
```

Iterators in Generic

Using the foreach construct is better known as iteration. If we have a customized generic class used as a list, and if we want to use foreach construct to iterate through the list, then the generic class has to implement the IEnumberable interface as shown below:

```
class mygenclass<T> : IEnumerable<T>
{
   T[] arr = new T[50];
   static int count = 0;
   public void Add(T item)
   {
      arr[count] = item;
      count++;
   }
   System.Collections.IEnumerator
System.Collections.IEnumerable.GetEnumerator()
   {
      for (int i = 0; i < arr.Length; i++)
      {
         yield return arr[i];
      }
   }
}
class Program
{
   static void Main(string[] args)
   {
      mygenclass<int> list = new mygenclass<int>();
      list.Add(10);
      list.Add(30);
      list.Add(20);
      foreach (int x in list)
      {WriteLine(x); }
   }
}
```

The IEnumerable Interface has a method called GetEnumerator which has to be implemented as shown above.

Chapter 9

Delegates

The function pointer in C was a reference to the entry point of a function and the concept was based on the address of the Function without any knowledge of the Signature.

So the function pointer was not type safe as it does not have any signature knowledge of the target Function. C# provides us with a similar feature like Function Pointer in C with a better safety – the delegate but how are they one step ahead of Function Pointers with minimal complexity?

What is a Delegate

A delegate is a type safe "Function Pointer", which is a reference to static or instance methods or functions. Delegates is one of the features of C# that works similar to C pointers but with added security and advantages. Delegates are mainly used in Event Handling.

Delegates are used to call methods dynamically at runtime.

Delegates are references to a method. Delegates are used to encapsulate references of method in delegate objects like class objects. Method invocation using delegate could be done at run time. At compile time, we don't need to provide complete information about referenced methods. We can reference methods according to need and invoke them by using the delegate at run time. The concept of the delegate is similar to function pointers used in C++; they are type safe and secure because methods which have same signature with the delegate type can only be called by delegate.

Delegate is the type of method rather than the class. Delegates are used to reference method instead of class.

For example: Employee EMP = new Employee ( ) ;

Here EMP is a reference to the Employee class type object. Like this, while instantiating delegate, we pass a method name to the delegate type. Example is in later section (instantiating a delegate).

Delegate types are derived from the System.Delegate class. The delegate's types are sealed. An instantiated delegate is an object; we can either assign it to a property or pass it as a parameter. This allows a delegate to be used as a parameter for a method. The delegate doesn't care or know about the class of the object that it references; all that matters is that the return type and arguments type of the method match with that of the delegate.

Now we need to know what type safe means and why we say that Delegates call functions dynamically. The next part talks about these points.

Delegate Declaration

Before using the delegate, we have to declare the it. Delegate declaration defines a type of method that is going to be encapsulating with a particular set of arguments and return type. For a different set of argument types or return value type, we have to declare a new delegate type.

In the following example, a delegate is declared, named Arithmetic, which encapsulates a method which takes two int type parameters and returns int.

public delegate int Arithmetic (int a, int b);

Instantiating a Delegate

Once we have declared a delegate type, we can set it to reference the actual method with a matching signature. A delegate reference can be created like an object reference.

Arithmetic mathsDelegate;

The delegate reference 'mathsDelegate' can now reference any method whose signature matches with the Arithmetic signature.

The delegate reference could be used to reference any method which has matching signature with declared delegate type by passing that method's name as parameter to the delegate type. Suppose we have a method which adds two numbers and return int value.

```
int Addition(int a, int b)
    {
    return a + b;
    }
    mathsDelegate = new Arithmetic(Addition);
```

Here, mathsDelegate is referring to Addition ( ) by passing its name to delegate type 'Arithmetic' as a parameter. Delegate instantiation is like all other objects using a new expression.

Arithmetic mathsDelegate = new Arithmetic(Addition);

Calling a Delegate

Once a delegate has been instantiated, the delegate object can be passed to some other piece of code for invoking the delegates. Once delegate has been invoked by using its object name, a method call will be passed to the referenced method. The parameters will be passed to the referenced method and return values will be passed to the point where the delegate had been invoked. We can call delegates either synchronously as per the example or asynchronously by using BEGININVOKE ( ) and ENDINVOKE ( ).

```
int C = mathsDelegate (10,20);
```

Delegates Example

//Declared outside the other classes as the declaration itself creates a new class named PrintDelegate

```
public delegate void PrintDelegate(String str);

class DelegateExample
{
    public static void PrintString(string str)
    {
        Console.WriteLine(str);

    }

    static void Main(string[] args)
    {
        PrintDelegate del = new PrintDelegate(PrintString);
        del("Hello World");

    }
}
```

public delegate void PrintDelegate (String str); - As given above, the line results in a new Delegate class creation with the name PrintDelegate which can call the methods that have one input parameter of type String and returns void (method with signature similar to delegate signature).

PrintDelegate del = new PrintDelegate (PrintString); -This line declares an object for the class PrintDelegate just like any normal class. We pass the method name (PrintString in this case) as the parameter and while compiling the signature of the method is matched with signature of our delegate. So PrintString is a method in the invocation list of the Delegate PrintDelegate.

del("Hello World"); -This is how we invoke the referenced methods in the invocation list of the delegate. The parameter given to the object is passed as the input parameter to the functions related to the Delegate.

So the function PrintString will be invoked with the input parameter "Hello World".

Singlecast and Multicast Delegate

When we reference or associate one single method/function to a delegate at a time, it's called SingleCast delegate. But we can reference multiple functions with a single delegate object, referred to as Multicast Delegates.

We can use the "+=" operator for adding the methods to multicast the delegate's invocation list, like this. "-=" is used for removing a method from the multicast delegate's invocation list.

In the example given above, we associated only one function (PrintString) with the Delegate (PrintDelegate) so that was an example for a SingleCast Delegate. But we can also associate multiple functions with a single delegate which is why they are known as Multicast Delegates.

Single Cast Delegate

```
using System;
using System.Collections.Generic;
using System.Linq;
using System.Text;

namespace Delegates
{
    public delegate double Arithmetic(double a, double b);  //Delegate
    Declaration

    public class Operations
    {
        public static double ADDITION(double a, double b)
        {
            return a + b;
        }

        public static double SUBSTRACTION(double a, double b)
        {
            return a - b;
        }

        public static double MULTIPLICATION(double a, double b)
        {
            return a * b;
        }

        public static double DIVIDE(double a, double b)
        {
            return a / b;}

public static double GREATEST(double a, double b)
```

```csharp
        {
            if (a > b)
                return a;
            else
                return b;
        }
    }

class Program
    {
        static void Main(string[] args)
        {
            Console.WriteLine("Which arithmetic operation you like to
            perform ");
            Console.WriteLine("Press + for ADD");
            Console.WriteLine("Press - for SUB");
            Console.WriteLine("Press * for MULTIPLY");
            Console.WriteLine("Press / for DEVIDE");
            Console.WriteLine("Press m for Greatest number");
            char choice = (char)Console.Read();
            DoAitrhmaticOperation(10, 20, choice);
        }

        static void DoAitrhmaticOperation(double a, double b, Char
        choice)
        {
            Arithmetic delegateAirthmatic = null;
            switch (choice)
            {
                case '+':
                    delegateAirthmatic = new
                    Arithmetic(Operations.ADDITION);
                    break;
```

```
    case '-':

    //Delegate Instantiation
    delegateAirthmatic = new Arithmetic(Operations.
    SUBSTRACTION);
        break;

    case '*':
        delegateAirthmatic = new Arithmetic(Operations.
        MULTIPLICATION);
        break;

    case '/':
        delegateAirthmatic = new
        Arithmetic(Operations.DIVIDE);
        break;

    case 'm':
        delegateAirthmatic = new
         Arithmetic(Operations.GREATEST);
        break;
    }

    double Z = delegateAirthmatic(a, b);  // calling or invoking a
    delegate

    Console.WriteLine("\n The result of arithmetic operation on
    a & b is: {0}", Z);
    }

  }
}
```

Multicast Delegate Example:

```
public delegate void CalculatorOperations(int x, int y);

    class MultiCastDelegate
    {

public static void Add(int x, int y) //Fun A with the same parameters
as Delegate
{
                Console.WriteLine("The sum is " + (x + y));
        }

        public static void Subtract(int x, int y) //Fun B with the same
        parameters as Delegate
        {
                Console.WriteLine("The subtraction is " + (x - y));
        }

        Static void Main(string[] args)
        {
            // Making the object of the Delegate class and adding the
            function Add to it
            CalculatorOperations cal = new
            CalculatorOperations(Add);
            cal(10,15);        // Calls the function Add with parameter
            10 and 15
            Console.WriteLine();

            cal += Subtract;     // Adding the other method Subtract
            with the delegate
            cal(15,20);        // Would call both the functions Add and
            Subtract with
            Console.WriteLine();      // parameters 15 and 20
```

```
        cal -= Add;        // Removing the other method Add
    from the delegate
    cal(20, 15);       // Would call only the functions Subtract
    with parameters
    Console.WriteLine();   // 20 and 15 as Add has been
    removed from the list


      }

 }
```

cal +=Subtract; - This way, we add any new method to the invocation list. Simply add the method name to the object of the delegate class.

cal -= Add; - This way, we remove any method to the invocation list. Simply subtract the method name from the object of the delegate class.

So we can add and remove any method any number of times from the Invocation List of a delegate.

So, the output for the program would be:

The sum is 25   --output of first delegate call

The sum is 35   --Output of second delegate call

The subtraction is -5

The subtraction is 5   --Output of third delegate call

Another example of multi Cast Delegate

```csharp
using System;
using System.Collections.Generic;
using System.Linq;
using System.Text;

namespace Delegates
{
  public delegate void InfoDelegate();

  public class Vehicle
  {
    public string strName;
    public string strType;
    public string strCompany;

    public Vehicle(string strName, string strType, string strCompany)
    {
      this.strName = strName;
      this.strType = strTypc;
      this.strCompany = strCompany;
    }

    public void ShowName()
    {
      Console.WriteLine("Name :" + this. strName);
    }

    public void ShowType()
    {
```

```csharp
            Console.WriteLine("Type :" + this. strType);
        }
public void ShowCompany()
        {
            Console.WriteLine("Company :" + this. strCompany);
        }
    }

class Program
    {

    static void Main(string[] args)
        {

        Vehicle vehc = new Vehicle("POLO", "Four Wheeler", "
        Volkswagen");

        InfoDelegate del = null;

        del = new InfoDelegate(vehc.ShowName);

        del += vehc.ShowType;   // Adding a method to delegate's
        invocation list

        del += vehc.ShowCompany;

        del(); // Will call all methods ShowName() and ShowType()
        and ShowCompany()

        Console.WriteLine("\After removing Last method");

        del -= vehc.ShowCompany; //Removing a method to
        delegate's invocation list
```

del(); // **Will call only two methods ShowName() and ShowType();**

Console.ReadLine();
        }
    }

}

OUTPUT:-

```
Name :POLO
Type :Four Wheeler
Company : Volkswagen

Aftetr removing Last method
Name :POLO
Type :Four Wheeler
```

Usage of Delegates

Now we know what delegates are, we need to know about their main usage. They are mainly used in Events.

Events

The simplest example of an Event is a Button Click. Most often, we see that when the save button is hit on a page, to stop the user from

121

making any more changes when the data is being saved, we freeze the screen during the save operation. So there is a class that is interested in the Save Button click to disable the screen controls. How is this class informed about the button click? Events do it for us. So an Event can be defined as:

"An Event in C# is a way by which a class notifies its clients when something interesting happens to that class."

So the main point is how events inform the client classes about the changes made to the controls or classes that are of their interest. This task is done by Delegates.

Events are actually declared using delegates. By the way of an event, a class allows its client to give the delegates to functions that should be called when the event occurs.

So in the example of a Save Button click, the client classes would have given the delegates that point to the functions that these client classes want to invoke on that button click.

Similarly, the events for a mouse can be Mouse Click, Mouse Hover and Mouse Move etc.

So events in C# work similar to our real world events. For example, in a UNESCO meeting, every country sends its delegates who inform their country about events of their interest. So the participating or interesting countries act like the client classes while the UN acts as the main class.

Practical Example:

After getting the insight of the Events, we will see a practical example.

A multinational company (MNC) has a couple of departments, namely the HR departments and the Worker department. The HR department co-ordinates the hiring process and, once they have employed a new worker, immediately the Worker department has to get a notification for planning the service details of the worker.

So whenever the HR department adds a new employee it wants to send his/her information to the Worker department.

So the participating classes are:

HR CLASS-acts as the primary class that raises the event when a new employee joins

Worker CLASS-acts as the client class that needs to be informed when a new employee joins

Please open the program in Visual Studio for better understanding.

Explanation for the HR class:

```
//Delegate Declaration outside all other classes as it also generates a
    separate class
    public delegate void NewEmpEventHandler(objcct sender,
    NewEmpEventArgs e);
//class HR that raises the event in case an Employee is added by the
    HR department
    class HRDept
```

```
{
    //Event of the type of delegates
    public event NewEmpEventHandler NewEmp ;

    protected virtual void WhenNewEmp(NewEmpEventArgs e)
    {
        //Checking that the Event Listener is not null
        if (NewEmp != null)
            NewEmp(this, e) ;
    }

    //Method to register a new employee
    public void EmpRegister(string name, int age, string sex)
    {
        NewEmpEventArgs e = new NewEmpEventArgs(name, age,
        sex) ;
        WhenNewEmpl( e ) ;
    }
}
```

NewEmpEventArgs is the class that we have declared which will be passed from HR to Worker class so it involves all those attributes that you want to pass from HR to Worker.

```
//Event declaration
public event NewEmpEventHandler NewEmp;
```

It will create an event named "NewEmp". The event is of the type of delegate so "NewEmpEventHandler" is the type of the event and NewEmp is its name.

Whenever this event is raised, it will invoke the delegate which will call the methods registered with it.

"WhenNewEmp" is a method that is called whenever a new employee is registered by the HR department. In method WhenNewEmp, we will raise the event with which the delegate of Child or interested classes (Worker class in this example) would be informed and they would invoke methods in their "Invocation list".

```
//Checking that the Event Listener is not null
 if (NewEmp != null)
      NewEmp(this, e);
```

The first line here checks that there is someone listening to the event raised.

If a listener is present, the second line raises the event.

Explanation for the Worker class:

```
// Worker class that would contain the event listener NewEmpAdded
   with the same signature as the delegate type
   class Worker
   {
// Constructor for Worker class that would add the event listener
   public Worker(HRDept hrdept)
   {
      hrdept.NewEmp += NewEmpAdded;
   }

   //Event Listener NewEmpAdded that would be called whenever
   the event NewEmp is published or raised
     private void NewEmpAdded(object sender, NewEmpEventArgs e)
```

```
        {
            Console.WriteLine(" Sent By: " + sender.ToString());
            Console.WriteLine(" Newly added Employee details: " +
        e.Name +
                        "," + e.Sex + "," + e.Age.ToString() ) ;
        }


    }


}
```

hrdept.NewEmp += NewEmpAdded; --This line adds the event listener called NewEmpAdded, which is actually a method that would be invoked whenever this event (NewEmp) is raised. NewEmpAdded method must have the signature similar to Delegate signature.

Inside the main method:

hrdept.EmpRegister("Mary", "Female", 25) ;

So when the method EmpRegister in Main is called, the series of events that take place is:

1. Inside EmpRegister we call OnNewEmp method

2. This method then checks the eventlisteners presence and raises the event NewEmp

3. NewEmp informs the registered class Worker and registered delegate of class ECC which invokes the method NewEmpAdded

4. This method then informs the ECC class the details of the new employee so by updating the class NewEmployeeEventArgs, you can add more details and it will be passed to Worker class whenever a new employee is registered by HRDept.

Chapter 10

Tuples

A tuple is a data structure containing a specific number and sequence of elements. It is already available in C#, Python and databases. The concept of Tuples is used in C# where it is used as a simple type that groups two or more values of any data type. Tuples were introduced with dynamic programming in C# 4.0. A tuple is an immutable, ordered sequence, fixed size of heterogeneous objects.

The order of the items in a tuple follows the same order followed at the time of creation. Neither the values of the tuples nor its size can be modified once it is created as the properties are read only and the tuple is of fixed size. Tuple types are very helpful for returning multiple values from functions, as it avoids the need to declare a new class or use references while writing a function that does some simple operation resulting in more returned values.

Insight into Tuple

In C#, a tuple is not a type. It is a static class that can hold multiple values. The class itself does not represent the tuples. Instead they have static methods known as helper methods that help us to create tuple objects without specifying the types explicitly. Tuples help us to display related data without having to create classes and properties. We can create a tuple either by using the constructor of the class or using the helper methods. However, using the constructor will make the code cumbersome.

Syntax to Create Tuple using the Constructor

Tuple<T> mytuple=new Tuple<T>(value1);

E.g.: Tuple<String> name= new Tuple<String>("C#");

So, to represent the marks and details of the student in a tuple we have to use the below code.

Tuple<string, int, int, int, int, int, int> student = new Tuple<string, int, int, int, int, int, int>("Jose", 123, 50, 60, 60, 76, 80);

Syntax to Create Tuple using the Helper Method Create

Tuple.Create(T1);

E.g.: var name= Tuple.Create("C#");

This an overloaded method. It can take one to eight parameters.

Different Types of Tuples

1. singleton
2. pair
3. triple
4. quadruple
5. quintuple
6. sextuple
7. septuple
8. octuple

However, there is a limitation in the number of objects supported by the .Net framework. It can support tuples with one to seven elements. To create tuples with eight or more elements, we have to nest a tuple object.

E.g.:

var odd = Tuple.Create(3, 5, 7,9, 11, 13, 15,17); // No error

var odd = Tuple.Create(3, 5, 7,9, 11, 13, 15,17,19); // Results in error

Hence the eight element should be represented as below

var odd = Tuple.Create(3, 5, 7,9, 11, 13, 15, Tuple.Create(17,19)) ;

How to Access the Elements in the Tuple

The elements in the tuple are immutable. Their values are initialized during the time of creation and once created they cannot be modified further. The values can be accessed using the attribute Item1, Item2 and so on.

E.g.:

Consider the tuple as below

var odd = Tuple.Create(3, 5, 7,9, 11, 13, 15, Tuple.Create(17,19)) ;

To get the value 7 to be printed, use **odd.Item3** as it is the third element in the list.

Tuple class has properties namely Item1, Item2... Item7; the rest belong to the respective elements. To access the eighth element, use **odd.Rest.Item1**

The output that will be displayed is (17, 19) as it is the eighth element in the tuple. In order to get only 17 to be printed, use **odd.Rest.Item1.Item1** and for 19 to be printed , use **odd.Rest.Item1.Item2**

Tuples do not have implicit meaning, as the elements are accessed using the property named Item. Although two tuples may have same set of elements their internal meaning might be different. The use of Tuple is generic and hence the developer should decide what it will mean during the time of creation and use.

Usage of Tuples

1. Return from the methods

    A function can always return only one value and whenever we need to return more than one value we make use of the **out** keyword to send the value. Instead, a tuple helps to combine multiple return values in a single variable and be sent out of the function.

2. Tuples can be used to represent the database records

3. Reduces the necessity to create a class or struct to carry a return from a method or to fill the list.

Let us consider a method that needs to takes two inputs and returns three output values; we can make use of tuple class in the method to accomplish the task.

```
public Tuple<double, double, double> Calculate(Tuple<int,
double> measure)
{
}
```

Comparison with Anonymous Types and KeyValue Pair

We can use an anonymous type to achieve the same task as we do with the help of tuples. But an anonymous type cannot be used as a return type in methods.

A tuple with two items will be faster compared to a key value pair type. A tuple takes more time for allocation compared to the

KeyValue pair. But whenever it is used as an argument to a method or a return value from a method or loaded from a list, the performance is very good compared to the KeyValue pair.

How to Store Tuples in a List

```
class Program
    {
        static void Main(string[] args)
        {

            List<Tuple<string, int>> studentlist = new List<Tuple<string,
            int>>();
            studentlist.Add(new Tuple<string, int>("Mary", 450));
            studentlist.Add(new Tuple<string, int>("Kevin",380));
            studentlist.Add(new Tuple<string, int>("Jack",430));

        }
    }
```

This example shows how to store the student details containing the name and the marks of the student in a list using a tuple. This student list resembles a database record.

Sorting a list with Tuples

In order to sort the list containing tuples, we can make use of sort method with the comparison delegate which sorts the entire list based on the item that is mentioned.

```
studentlist.Sort((a, b) => a.Item2.CompareTo(b.Item2));
```

```
foreach (var student in studentlist)
{
    Console.WriteLine(student.Item1 + "   " + student.Item2);
}
```

The result is the sorted list based on the marks of the student (in ascending order). So the output will look like below.

Kevin   380

Jack   430

Mary   450

Working with a Database Record

Tuples mainly help to represent the database record. Consider that we are working with a web application and the application follows an architecture where all the database records are returned as list elements with the help of entities. Whenever the data fetched belongs to a single table, it can be represented by a single entity. Instead, for a particular report, when you need to fetch data from more than one table, it becomes unnecessary to create a new class or entity only for this purpose. Tuples reduce the necessity to create a class or struct to carry a return from a method or to fill the list.

Let us consider the database has two tables, namely Employee and Department.

Department (DeptId, DepartmentName)

Employee(EmployeeId,EmployeeName,Designation,DeptId)

Each of these tables can be represented as a class with the fields being the properties of the class.

If we need to fetch a report, which displays the employee details along with the department details, we should write a join query. In this case, to represent the result in the frontend we cannot join two classes. Also it is not advisable to create a new class containing the required fields combined from both the tables just for the purpose of report. So Tuples can be used to represent the database record.

Although tuples do not have an explicit meaning and make the code unreadable, they are very useful whenever we want to pass more than one value or retrieve more than one value from a method. We can also use it to represent database records in our code without having to create a class or struct to store them. It is very useful for storing conceptual data and always can be considered as a better option when compared to using KeyValue pair type.

Chapter 11

Interfaces

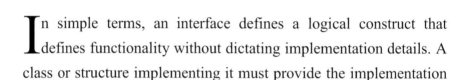

In simple terms, an interface defines a logical construct that defines functionality without dictating implementation details. A class or structure implementing it must provide the implementation details.

In order to define an interface, let us take the example of a builder hiring 3 different contractors.

Say a builder 'A' wants to build three apartments at nearby locations. He hires three contractors and gives them the contract of building one apartment each using a similar architectural plan. Now the contractors have to abide by the contract of the plan given by the builder. However, it is entirely down to them which raw materials to use, which color to use for painting the walls, type of flooring to use, etc.

Hence, an interface can be defined as a deal or contract, i.e. the architectural plan in the above example, and the classes implementing the interface, i.e. the builders in the above the case, should abide by the contract or deal but can provide implementation of the methods in the interface depending on their individual requirements.

Interfaces and Abstract Classes

An abstract method defines the signature of the method without provision of any proper implementation in a base class. A derived class must provide its own implementation of each abstract method defined in its base class.

However, by using interfaces in C#, a class interface can be formed entirely separated from its implementation.

Syntactically, interfaces are similar to abstract classes.

Unlike abstract classes, in an interface no method can include implementation.

An interface can be implemented by any number of classes and each class can define its own functionality for the methods, properties, etc.

Basically, an interface is to be used when the concept of a requirement can be defined in terms of what needs to be done, leaving aside the implementation details. However, when the requirement demands inclusion of certain implementation details, abstract classes should be used.

An interface can be of immense help in case of a pluggable component architecture in which the functionality can be made to abide by the contract defined by the interfaces, and also in case of *AbstractFactory* design pattern.

Using Interfaces

1. Once an interface has been defined, it can be implemented by one or more classes. An interface is declared by using the keyword *interface* and the general form of a class implementing an interface is:

```
class class_name : interface_name
{
        //class body
        public void WriteString()
        {
          Console.WriteLine( "This is an example of interface
implementation" );
        }
}
```

2. When a class implements an interface, it must implement the entire interface. It cannot exclude implementation of some parts of the interface.

3. *Example:*

Let us explain the usage of interfaces by a simple example.

Suppose there is a requirement to print all numbers 1 to *i* where *i* is a variable, and to print *i* number of multiples of *i* . For example if i = 5, print numbers from 1 to 5 and 5 multiples of 5 as 5, 10, 15, 20, 25.

Let us use the concept of interfaces to accomplish the above requirement.

1. Open a new Visual Studio project.

2. Add four classes *ISimpleInterface.cs*, *UseSimpleInterface1.cs*, *UseSimpleInterface2.cs* and *Execute.cs*.

3. Include the following code for *ISimpleInterface.cs*:

```
using System;
namespace CSharp.SimpleInterfaceExample
{
        public interface ISimpleInterface
        {
                void PrintNumbers( int i );
                void PrintString( string s );
        }
}
```

Explanation: The above chunk of code declares an interface *ISimpleInterface* which contains two methods, *PrintNumbers* and *PrintString*, to be implemented by the classes implementing *ISimpleInterface*.

4. In order to achieve the functionality of printing all numbers from 1 to i and printing a user –friendly string, implement *UseSimpleInterfce1.cs* as shown below:

```
using System;
namespace CSharp.SimpleInterfaceExample
{
        /// <summary>
        /// This class implements ISimpleInterface.
        /// </summary>
        public class UseSimpleInterface1 : ISimpleInterface
        {
                /// <summary>
                /// This method print all the numbers from one to i.
                /// </summary>
                /// <param name="i">An integer.</param>
                public void PrintNumbers( int i )
                {
                        for( int j = 1; j <= i; j++ )
                        {
                                Console.WriteLine( "Printing Number {0}",
                                        j );
                        }
                }
                /// <summary>
                /// This method prints a string.
                /// </summary>
                /// <param name="s">A string.</param>
                public void PrintString( string s )
                {
```

```
                    Console.WriteLine( "Print Numbers with
                    " + s +" implementation" );
               }
          }
}
```

Explanation: *UseSimpleInterface1*   class   implements
ISimpleInterface. Hence, as per the concept of interface
implementation, it should provide functionality for all the
methods defined in the interface i.e. *PrintNumbers* and
PrintString. In this case, *PrintNumbers* method on invocation
will print numbers from 1 to *i* depending on the parameter '*i*'
and *PrintString* will print a string depending on the value of the
parameter '*s*'.

5. In order to achieve the functionality of printing the multiple of 5
    and printing a user – friendly string, implement
    UseSimpleInterface1.cs as shown below:

```
using System;
namespace CSharp.SimpleInterfaceExample
{
     /// <summary>
     /// This class implements ISimpleInterface.
     /// </summary>
     public class UseSimpleInterface2 : ISimpleInterface
     {
          /// <summary>
          /// This method prints 'i' multiples of i.
          /// </summary>
```

```
/// <param name="i">An integer.</param>
public void PrintNumbers( int i )
{
        for( int j = 1; j <= i; j++ )
        {
                Console.WriteLine(       "Printing
                Number {0}", i * j );
        }
}
/// <summary>
/// This method prints a string.
/// </summary>
/// <param name="s">A string.</param>
public void PrintString( string s )
{
                Console.WriteLine( "Print
                Numbers with "
                    + s + " implementation" );
        }
    }
}
```

Explanation: *UseSimpleInterface2* class implements *ISimpleInterface*. Hence, as per the concept of the interface implementation, it should provide functionality for all the methods defined in the interface i.e. *PrintNumbers* and *PrintString*. In this case, the PrintNumbers method on invocation will result in *i* number of multiples of i depending on the parameter '*i*' and *PrintString* will print a string depending on the value of the parameter '*s*'.

6. After implementing the interfaces as per the requirement, now it's time to invoke the implemented methods which can be accomplished by implementing *Execute.cs;* this contains the main entry point for the application as shown in the following code snippet:

```
using System;
namespace CSharp.SimpleInterfaceExample
{
        /// <summary>
        /// Executes the application.
        /// </summary>
        public class Execute
        {
                public static void Main( string[] args )
                {
                        UseSimpleInterface1 obj1
                        = new UseSimpleInterface1();
                        obj1.PrintString( "UseSimpleInterface1" );
                        obj1.PrintNumbers( 5 );
                        UseSimpleInterface2 obj2
                        = new UseSimpleInterface2();
                        obj2.PrintString( "UseSimpleInterface2" );
                        obj2.PrintNumbers( 5 );
                        Console.ReadLine();
                }
        }
}
```

Explanation: *Execute.cs* consists of the main method which serves as the entry of the application. In this method, two instances of the respective classes are created and the respective methods of the classes are invoked.

7. Compile and run the application. The following output is generated:

Output

Print Numbers with UseSimpleInterface1 implementation
Printing Number 1
Printing Number 2
Printing Number 3
Printing Number 4
Printing Number 5
Print Numbers with UseSimpleInterface2 implementation
Printing Number 5
Printing Number 10
Printing Number 15
Printing Number 20
Printing Number 25

Classes Implementing more than one Interface

It is permissible for classes to use more than one interface. To implement more than one interface, each must be separated with commas.

A class can also inherit a base class and implement more than one interface. In such a scenario, the base class should be included first in the comma – separated list.

A class that implements more than one interface must implement all the methods, properties and events of all the implemented interfaces.

Interface References

The concept of interfaces in C# has support for the usage of interface reference variables. Such a variable can refer to any object that implements its interface. When a method is invoked on an object through an interface reference, it is the version of the method implemented by the object that is executed.

The above concept of interface reference is illustrated by the following example:

Example: Suppose there is product "SOAP". Let "Lux" be the distinguishing category and all other brands fall into the second category. Suppose the requirement is to calculate the rate of an item of "SOAP". Let there be two algorithms *'AlgorithmLux'* and *'AlgorithmAll'* to calculate the rate depending on the location of procurement of the product. If the location is Delhi, then *'AlgorithmLux'* would be used otherwise the latter would be taken into account. Carry out the following steps to in order to accomplish the requirement:

1. Create a Console application with four classes - *IProductRate.cs*, *Execute.cs*, *AlgorithmAll.cs* and *AlgorithmLux.cs*.

2. Add the following code snippet to *IProductRate.cs*:

145

```csharp
using System;
namespace CSharp.Interface.ProductRate
{
    /// <summary>
    /// This is an interface.
    /// </summary>
    public interface IProductRate
    {
        double CalculateRate( string itemName );
    }
}
```

Explanation: IProductRate is an interface containing a method *CalculateRate* to be implemented by classes intending to perform rate calculation for an item specified by the parameter *'itemName'*.

3. Add the following code snippet to *AlgorithmLux.cs*:

```csharp
using System;
namespace CSharp.Interface.ProductRate
{
    /// <summary>
    /// This class calculates the rate of a product item.
    /// </summary>
    public class AlgorithmLux :    IProductRate
    {
        public double CalculateRate( string itemName )
        {
            switch( itemName.ToUpper() )
            {
                case "LUX":
                    return 25.00;
```

```
                    default:
                          return 20.00;
                 }
              }
          }
}
```

Explanation: The *AlgorithmLux* class implements *IProductRate* interface and provides implementation of the method *CalculateRate* to perform rate calculation for an item specified by the parameter *'itemName'*. If an item is "LUX", it returns "25.00" else it returns "20.00".

4. Add the following code snippet to *AlgorithmAll.cs*:

```
using System;
namespace CSharp.Interface.ProductRate
{
        /// <summary>
        /// This class calculates the rate of a product item.
        /// </summary>
        public class AlgorithmAll :     IProductRate
        {
               public double CalculateRate( string itemName )
               {
                      return 21.00;
               }
        }
}
```

Explanation: The *AlgorithmAll* class implements the *IProductRate* interface and provides implementation of the method *CalculateRate* to perform rate calculation for an item specified by the parameter *'itemName'*. It returns the calculated rate as "21.00" irrespective of the item name.

5. Add the following code snippet to Execute.cs:

```csharp
using System;

namespace CSharp.Interface.ProductRate
{
        /// <summary>
        /// This class illustrates the usage of interface reference.
        /// </summary>
        class Execute
        {
                /// <summary>
                /// The main entry point for the application.
                /// </summary>
                [STAThread]
                static void Main( string[] args )
                {
                        //Create a reference variable of IProductRate.
                        string sLocation = "Delhi";
                        IProductRate obj;
                        obj = new AlgorithmLux();
                        if( sLocation.ToUpper().Equals( "DELHI" ) )
                        {
                                Console.WriteLine( "Price of Lux Soap"
                                        + " in Delhi is: "
                                        + obj.CalculateRate( "LUX" ) );
                                Console.WriteLine( "Price of all other"
                                        + " soaps in Delhi is: "
                                        + obj.CalculateRate( "All") );
```

```
            }
        obj = new AlgorithmAll();
        Console.WriteLine( "Price of Lux Soap in rest "
                + "of India other than Delhi is: "
                + obj.CalculateRate( "LUX" ) );
        Console.WriteLine( "Price of all other soaps"
                + " in rest"
                + "of India other than Delhi is: "
                + obj.CalculateRate( "All") );
        Console.ReadLine();
        }
    }
}
```

Explanation: In the *Main* method in the code snippet above, a reference variable of *IProductRate* is declared. This means it can be used to store references to any object that implements *IProductRate*. In this case, it is used to hold references to *AlgorithmLux* and *AlgorithmAll*, both of which implement IProductRate.

6. Compile and run the application. The following output is generated:

Output:

Price of Lux Soap in Delhi is: 25
Price of all other soaps in Delhi is: 20
Price of Lux Soap in rest of India other than Delhi is: 21
Price of all other soaps in rest of India other than Delhi is: 21

Limitation of interface reference variable:

An interface reference variable has knowledge only of the methods declared by its interface declaration. Hence such an object cannot be used to access any other variables or methods that might be supported by the object.

Interface Properties, Events and Indexers

Like methods, properties, events and indexers can also be specified in an interface without a body.

Interface Inheritance:

One interface can inherit another interface. When a class implements an interface which, in turn inherits another interface, it must provide implementations for all the members defined within the interface inheritance chain, otherwise a compile-time error would result.

Usage of new keyword with interface inheritance:

Taking into account interface inheritance, it is possible to declare a member in the derived interface than hide one defined in the base interface. Basically, such a scenario comes into play when a member in the derived interface has the same signature as in the base interface. This would generate a warning message and can be overcome by modifying the derived interface member with the *new* keyword.

Explicit Interface Implementations:

A member of an interface can be implemented with its fully qualified name i.e. with the interface name.

Such an implementation is termed as *"Explicit Interface Implementation"* and is encouraged during the following scenarios:

1. When the requirement is to provide private implementation that is not exposed to outside classes.

2. To resolve the ambiguity which arises when a class implements two or more interfaces with the same signature for one or methods.

The following code snippet illustrates the usage of explicit implementation of interface members.

```
using System;
namespace CSharp.Interface.ProductRate
{
        /// <summary>
        /// An interface to demonstrate explicit interface
        /// member implementation.
        /// </summary>
        public interface IExplicitImplementation
        {
                void PrintString( string sPrint );
        }

        /// <summary>
        /// A class implementing IExplicitImplementation interface.
```

```
/// </summary>
class ImplementInterface : IExplicitImplementation
{
        /// <summary>
        /// This method illustrates explicit implementation of
        /// interface member PrintString.
        /// </summary>
        /// <param name="sPrint">The string to be
        printed.</param>
        void IExplicitImplementation.PrintString( string sPrint )
        {
                Console.WriteLine( sPrint );
        }
        /// <summary>
        /// The main entry point of the application.
        /// </summary>
        [STAThread]
        static void Main( string[] args )
        {
           IExplicitImplementation obj = new
        ImplementInterface();
           obj.PrintString( "This is an example" +
                        " of Explicit implementation of an "
                        + "interface member" );
           Console.ReadLine();
        }
}
}
```

Limitations of interfaces in C#:

1. Interfaces cannot include data members.

2. Interfaces cannot define constructors, destructors and operator methods.

3. No member of an interface can be declared as static.

4. A class implementing an interface must implement the entire interface.

5. An interface reference variable can only access the methods declared by its interface declaration.

Chapter 12

Static Class

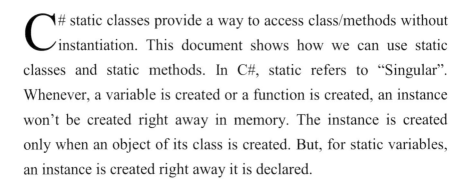

C# static classes provide a way to access class/methods without instantiation. This document shows how we can use static classes and static methods. In C#, static refers to "Singular". Whenever, a variable is created or a function is created, an instance won't be created right away in memory. The instance is created only when an object of its class is created. But, for static variables, an instance is created right away it is declared.

Static classes can be used in methods, classes, fields, properties, operator, constructors and events. Usage of a static class comes into the picture when information needs to be applicable to an entire class. So, static classes cannot access non-static members. Creation of the static keyword makes the code work a bit faster. Static members belong to that particular class and not to any object of the class.

Static classes are used in situations where methods are not related\associated with particular objects. It helps the programmer to keep the method inside class in a simple yet meaningful way.

Features

1. Static class is a class which can be accessed without instantiation.
2. Static class contains only static members.
3. Static class cannot be instantiated.
4. Static class cannot be inherited.
5. Static class contain instance constructor.
6. Static classes are sealed by default.
7. Static class groups related static members
8. Static class is sealed (It cannot be inherited).

Example:

```
static class Shape
{
   public static double Area(double width, double height)
   {
      return width * height;
   }
}

class rectangle
{
   Main()
   {
//shape class is accessed without instantiation
```

Console.Writeline("Area:{0}", **Shape**.Area(5,6));
  }
}

Now let us see the usage of Static/Non static methods in same class or different class.

Non Static Methods Inside Same Class

In this scenario, if a method has to be called, its class should be instantiated and then, using the object of its class, we can call the method even though that method is in the same class. Non-static class cannot be called without creating instance of the class. So, non-static methods always need the instance of the class. An object of the class is required to access its method.

Example:

```
class program
  {
    public int Calc(int x, int y)
      {
        return x * y;
      }
    Main()
      {
        Program x = new program();
        Console.Writeline(x.Calc(6, 5)); //needs instantiation
      }
  } // End of class program
```

Static Methods Inside Same Class

In this scenario, the static method can be called without instantiating the class, as shown in following example. Here, the class program is not instantiated while calling it from Main(). So, there is no need to instantiate the program class for calling a static method, "Calc", inside the same class.

```
class program
{
    public static  int Calc(int x, int y) //usage of static keyword
    {
        return x * y;
    }
    Main()
    {
        // No instantiation required
        Console.Writeline(Calc(6, 5));
    }
} // End of class program
```

Static Method between different Classes

In this scenario, there is no need to instantiate the class, though the method is in a different class as shown in following example. A static method does not require any class object. So, the static method is shared amongst all instances of the class. A method that is marked as static can be accessed from all instances of that class through the class *name*:

```
class program
{
    public static int Calc(int x, int y) // usage of static keyword
    {
        return x * y;
    }
}//End of class program

class MainClass
{
    Main()
    {
        // No instantiation required
        Console.Writeline(Program.Calc(6, 5));
    }
} //End of Mainclass
```

All the above three programs gives same output - "30". Non static methods inside same class need the class to be instantiated, whereas a static method inside same class/different class does not needs to be instantiated.

Static Constructors

It is used to initialize the static fields with a type. A static constructor can be declared for the static instance just like a constructor for a normal instance.

```
class program
{
    static readonly int val;
```

```
static program ()
{
    val = 9;
}

} // End of Mainclass
```

Chapter 13

Background Worker in C#

Introduction

This chapter covers the use of the BackgroundWorker class in a C# based application and how to achieve multithreading using the same.

When a GUI rich application includes lengthy database transactions there are chances that the UI may appear blocked till the control returns from accessing the database. This is because the same thread which is accessing the database cannot draw the UI too. To avoid this, one can go for multithreading where the UI thread continues with (re)drawing and other UI activities and have another individual dedicated thread for database transactions.

In such scenarios, the BackgroundWorker class comes handy. On instantiating this class, a separate thread is spawned which works **asynchronous**[1] to the calling thread. In the above case, all the database transactions can be done by this background thread, while the main thread (the UI thread) continues with its sequence of execution unabated.

The BackgroundWorker class belongs to the namespace System.ComponentModel. This is the most appropriate one to be put to use in those situations when time-consuming jobs such as database transactions, web uploading etc., are involved in an application.

Multithreading can be achieved in an application (C#) in three ways. They are

1. Using Thread class belonging to (System.Threading namespace)

2. Using the methods BeginInvoke() and Invoke() in a form(a derivative of System.Windows.Forms class).

3. Using BackgroundWorker class

Let us see merits and demerits of them.

Using Thread Class

- Using the System.Threading.Thread class involves compelling coding for creating threads, restarting logic in case of pausing the thread, suspension of the same, handling synchronization problems etc.

- Threads spawned using 'Thread' class are synchronous in nature. i.e. the calling thread waits for the return of the called thread. So this may not be very efficient in supporting simultaneous tasks where are both are time-consuming.

- Simple to create.

Using BeginInvoke() and Invoke() Methods

- These two methods use threads from the system's thread pool. A maximum of 25 threads can be used at any instance of time.

- The lifespan and synchronization of created threads is handled by the system.

- The BeginInvoke() method executes in an asynchronous way with respect to the called thread whereas thread spawned using the Invoke() method is synchronous to the called party.

- Both the methods 'delegate' the task to other methods for execution.

- Threads spawned using these are not to be suspended or paused.

- Once threads are created, the main way of communication with the called thread is through methods/delegates. There is no default mechanism to know the status of the delegated task.

Using BackgroundWorker Class

- A dedicated class provided by Microsoft Visual Studio 2005 that spawns asynchronous threads.

- Simple to use.

- Members of this class provide lots of features, such as to report the progress of the delegated task (through *ProgressChanged* **event[2]**), to interrupt/terminate the created thread.

- System handles the lifespan and synchronization of created threads.

- Apt for time-consuming jobs.

With this broad know-how of each of the methods let us get to know in detail of the method we employed in our project.

In this chapter, I would like to explain how this BackgroundWorker class was deployed in our project. Ours was a GUI based application developed in C# - a one-stop utility to install various products of our client on to the systems. Here installation refers to creating a product database, creating tables and views in it, loading of several stored procedures, updating tables etc. It was database driven utility and was time consuming. We also had to cater to the client's requirement of installing more than one product simultaneously.

So we used the approach of instantiating a BackgroundWorker class to execute this task of installation – which includes establishing connection with the product database and creating tables and other database related time-consuming transactions.

We also used the BeginInvoke() and Invoke() methods to delegate UI related functionalities.

This chapter throws light on the use of the BackgroundWorker class only.

We have a form (a derivative of System.Windows.Forms class) which is rich in GUI controls. It has a few buttons, labels, Datagrid, checkboxes and pictures.

On selecting to install a product, its installation commences. At this point in time, a connection to that product's database is to be established and database transactions would begin. Since this is a time-consuming job, this blocked our UI. So at this instance, a BackgroundWorker is instantiated immediately.

BackgroundWorker is available in the ToolBox window in the Visual Studio IDE. It can be dragged and dropped on to the form. It can also be used by declaring snd instantiating as shown below.

BackgroundWorker bgwProductInstaller = new BackgroundWorker();

bgwProductInstaller.WorkerSupportsCancellation = true;

WorkerSupportsCancellation is a property which specifies if asynchronous cancellation is supported or not. If this is set to true, then this background worker can be interrupted and terminated (if needed).

bgwProductInstaller.WorkerReportsProgress = true;

WorkerReportsProgress is a property which specifies if this background worker can report progress updates. When this is set to true, it helps in intimating the progress of execution of the task quantified in terms of percentage of work done.

This diagram depicts the overall sequence of flow of execution between the main (UI) thread and the Worker thread

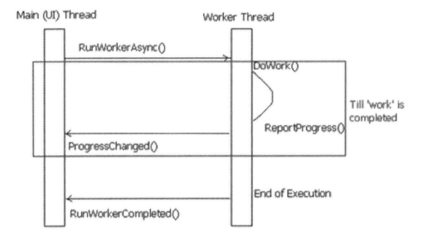

Main (UI) Thread Worker Thread

RunWorkerAsync()

DoWork()

Till 'work' is completed

ReportProgress()

ProgressChanged()

End of Execution

RunWorkerCompleted()

bgwProductInstaller.DoWork += new

   DoWorkEventHandler(ProductInstallationForm_DoWork);

DoWork is an action which is handled by *DoWorkEventHandler.* The method, *ProductInstallationForm_DoWork()* contains the code for installation. This is a declaration statement which defines that, on raise of the event *'Do Work,'* control shifts to the method *ProductInstallationForm_DoWork()* and execution of the code happens in a new thread.

Now let us see what would raise the *'Do Work'* event.

bgwProductInstaller.RunWorkerAsync();

Calling this method, *RunWorkerAsync()* calls the event handler, *ProductInstallationForm_DoWork().* At this instance, the 'work' defined in this method, is executed in a separate thread, which runs at the background of the main (UI) thread. The created thread runs asynchronous to the calling thread. i.e. the main thread does not wait for background thread's return to continue its flow of execution.

```
ProductInstallationForm_DoWork(object sender, DoWorkEventArgs e)
{
/*Code for installing our client's product - to access the database,
create a new one, create tables, update them etc. */
bgwProductInstaller.ReportProgress(25) ;
/*Further Code to access database */
bgwProductInstaller.ReportProgress(35) ;
}
```

Creating a database and all those database related transactions are running in a separate thread at the background, without blocking the UI. Notice the statement where the method, *ReportProgress()* is called.

Calling ReportProgress raises the *ProgressChanged()* event. Numbers 25 and 35 denote the percentage of completion. This can range from 0 to 100. At any point of time during the course of a background work, progress of the work can be reported.

In the event handler, *ProgressChanged()*, we can display the progress through a progress bar or, after coming to know the progress, we can decide on further flow of execution.

Here I have used a progress bar (prgInstallation) to display the progress of installation

ProductInstallationForm_ProgressChanged(object sender, ProgressChangedEventArgs e)
{
prgInstallation.Value = e.ProgressPercentage ;
}

A *RunWorkerCompleted()* event is triggered, when the *DoWork()* event handler returns – either due to completion of the work, or because of cancellation of the job or because of an exception thrown.

Follow this link to know more about this event:

http://msdn2.microsoft.com/en-us/library/system.componentmodel.backgroundworker.runworkercompleted.aspx

The requirement in our project was to handle installation of more than one product simultaneously. So, we used an array of BackgroundWorker for concurrent installation giving our application a multi-threaded approach. Each BackgroundWorker would be installing individual products. In this way, the main (UI) thread and 'n' number of background threads run asynchronously to each other giving the application a non-blocking smooth execution.

Chapter 14

Multithreading in C#

For a long time, most of the applications were single threaded which meant the entire application had only one thread and that single thread used to do all the work for that process. The process can start other actions only after the running thread finishes its execution, which results in system idle time. With the introduction of multithreading, a process can have multiple threads and the different threads can do different tasks simultaneously, which increases the system performance and the responsiveness to the user.

Synchronization between the threads is highly important since multiple threads try to access the same object and this may result in inconsistency. In .Net, synchronization is achieved by using Monitor class and Lock statements. Interthread communication is done by using Wait(), Pulse() and PulseAll() methods defined in the Monitor class. They should be called from the block of code which is locked otherwise a SynchronizationLockException will be thrown.

Using multiple threads in an application sometimes reduces the speed of the application. Tracking and switching between multiple threads consumes more CPU time and memory resources. Hence it is not always preferable to use multiple threads in an application.

Introduction to Threads

Any Application/Program running in the system is a process and each process may consist of one or more threads. A thread is a smallest unit and separate stream of execution where the OS can allocate processor time. The Main() thread is the entry point of all the programs as execution starts with the first statement in the Main() method and continues until that method returns.

A process with one thread is called a Single Threaded Application and more than one thread is a Multi-threaded Application.

Single Threaded Application

If a process contains only one thread which does all the work for the process, it is considered as a Single threaded application.

Disadvantages of Single Threaded Application – Main () Thread

- All the work will be done by only one thread within the process
- The process can continue with other actions only after the current thread finishes its execution.

- Results in system idle time which in turn degrades the system performance.

Multithreading

Multithreading makes use of separate additional threads for time consuming tasks instead of using the main application thread. The OS allocates processor time to threads, so a process with multiple threads gets more CPU time than the usual share.

For example, consider a time-consuming function (like retrieving millions of records from the database) that needs to be called as a response of a button click. Since it takes a lot of time to retrieve huge number of records, the application freezes while waiting for the function to finish execution. To avoid this, create a new thread and assign the time consuming function to the newly created thread. The Main thread continues to perform the other tasks while the newly created thread runs in the background executing the time consuming task. Therefore the application interface will not be blocked and the performance and responsiveness of the application improves as the two threads run in parallel.

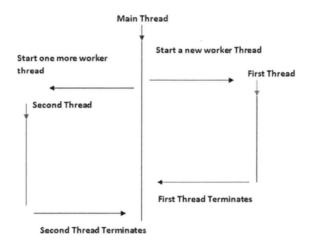

Fig 1: Multithreading Scenario

In Fig 1, the Main thread (which is the first thread) starts its execution. This thread can start any number of worker threads.

The program execution splits into two once a new thread is started. The statements following the starting of a new thread will get some CPU time and some goes into the method associated with the new thread. Determining which statements will run first is totally unpredictable as mostly they get intermixed.

Any number of threads can be started. They will continue executing their own execution path.

Advantages of Multithreading

The main advantages of multithreading are:

- Program's responsiveness to the user.

- Improvement of application's performance

Generally, multithreading in .Net can be in two ways:

- ThreadStart delegates are created by the user to start their own threads. These manually created threads are preferred for time taking tasks.

- ThreadPool class is generally preferred for short tasks. This class can be used from ThreadPool.QueueUserWorkItem or Stream.BeginRead method, or BeginInvoke method. Stream.BeginRead and BeginInvoke methods are asynchronous methods.

Creating Threads using ThreadStart Delegate

A new thread is created through ThreadStart delegate in the following way:

```
Using System.Threading;
ThreadStart ts=new ThreadStart(TestMethod);
Thread t1=new Thread(ts);
T1.Name= "NewThread";
t1.Start();
public void TestMethod()
{
    // Does some computation
}
```

System.Threading namespace contains the definition for Thread class and ThreadStart delegate.

Every thread has to be associated with a method to execute. Here, TestMethod is the one associated with the newly created thread. This is done by creating an object of ThreadStart delegate, after this object is created we have created an object of Thread class.

The constructor of Thread class accepts one parameter – ThreadStart delegate object. The name property of Thread t1 has been set to "NewThread". We have used Start() method to begin the execution of thread t1. After the Start() method is invoked, the execution of Main thread and thread t1 gets intermixed. The OS takes care of switching between the threads.

In .Net 1.1, the thread entry point cannot take any parameters and cannot return anything. But .Net 2.0 allows passing a parameter to the function which is associated with the thread. In that case, we need to use a ParameterizedThreadStart delegate instead of ThreadStart delegate.

Creating a Thread using Parameterized ThreadStart Delagate

```
ParameterizedThreadStart ts = new ParameterizedThreadStart
(TestMethod);
Thread t1 = new Thread (ts);
T1.Name= "NewThread";
t1.Start();
public void TestMethod(object pobjobject)
{
    // Does some computation
}
```

Thread States

The current state of a thread can be determined through the ThreadStart property, which returns a ThreadState enumeration number. The various enumeration members are listed below:

- Aborted – The thread has been stopped due to an abort request.

- AbortRequested – Another thread has requested that this thread be terminated.

- BackGround – The thread is executing as a background thread.

- Running – The thread is executing or eligible for execution by OS.

- Stopped – The thread has stopped executing.

- StopRequested – The thread has been requested to stop.

- Suspended – The thread is suspended.

- SuspendRequested – Another thread has requested that this thread be suspended.

- Unstarted - The thread has been created but has not yet started.

- WaitSleepJoin – The thread has been blocked while waiting for another object to be signaled, has called sleep, or is waiting to join another thread.

Synchronization

When working with multiple threads, Synchronization is the crucial aspect as they compete for shared resources. Multiple threads compete for shared objects such as instance variables, Database connections, GUI controls and devices. Inconsistency will result when one thread is changing the state of an object and another thread tries to read the same object. To avoid this, threads needs to be synchronized.

Through Synchronization, critical sections of the code are locked and only one thread can get the lock at one time and other threads gets blocked and have to wait. The locks have to be released otherwise deadlock can result.

Threads Synchronization in .Net:

Thread Synchronization in .Net can be obtained through Monitor class or Lock statement.

Monitor Class

In .Net framework, the **Monitor** class (Sealed class) is used for Synchronization. A block of code which is accessed by many threads is called a critical section. If more than one thread accesses the critical section at the same time, it results in inconsistency. To avoid this inconsistency, the Monitor class provides a lock on the critical section to a single thread at a time. Once a thread acquires a lock on the critical section, no other thread is allowed to enter that section. Other threads have to wait till this thread releases the lock.

Features of Monitor class:

- Monitor class does not grant locks on all objects. It grants locks on objects only if the object demands for it.

- Instance cannot be created for a Monitor class.

Each synchronized object maintains the following information:

- Only one thread can acquire a lock on an object at any one time. A reference to this thread is maintained.

- Threads that are waiting to acquire the lock are placed in a queue called the ready queue. A reference to this queue is maintained.

- Threads need to be notified about the change in the locked object state. All these threads are placed in the waiting queue. A reference to this queue is maintained.

Monitor class has 3 methods: Entry, Exit and TryEnter

Monitor.Enter(this);

Monitor.Exit(this);

If(!(Montor.TryEnter(this))

Return false;

Lock statement

The "Lock" keyword helps in marking a block of statements as a critical section. This statement ensures that one thread does not enter the critical section while another thread is executing.

Let's consider a simple example where we use Monitor for synchronization:

```
Public void TestMethod()
{
int x = 10;
int y = 0;
Monitor.Enter(this);
int z = x / y;
Monitor.Exit(this);
}
```

The above code will face problems in the program execution. As soon as the control flow comes to the statement z = x / y, an exception will be thrown and thus Monitor.Exit(this) function will be skipped by .NET and the program will hang because none of the other threads can acquire lock.

To handle scenarios like this, we can use below points.

- Always write the code in a try, catch and finally block and then call the Monitor.Exit function in finally block. This will ensure the lock gets removed because the finally block will get executed irrespective of any exception which might arise in the program.

- C# provides lock() method. Using lock(this) as well as Monitor.Enter(this) are both equal in nature.

Lock () and Monitor are almost similar, but lock is the short way of acquiring monitor and making sure it gets freed again. Therefore

```
lock(obj)
{
}
is equivalent to
Monitor.Enter(obj)
try
{
// Critical code
}
finally
{
Monitor.Exit(obj)
}
```

InterThread Communication

Threads need to communicate with each other while

- Waiting for a shared resource to get released.

- In the producer consumer model, notifying other threads if some new work arrives.

- Waiting for the clients in the network server model.

- An application event has finished.

Monitor class defines three methods Wait(), Pulse() and PulseAll() methods to support interthread communication. They should be called from the section where the block of code is locked else SynchronizationLockException will be thrown.

The Wait() method of Monitor class is called when a thread is temporarily stopped from running. The thread goes to a sleep state and releases the lock, so that another thread can enter the critical section. When some other thread enters the critical section, the Pulse() or PulseAll() methods are called by this thread to awaken the sleeping threads. The first thread waiting in the queue is resumed by calling Pulse() method. The PulseAll() method is called to awaken all the threads waiting in the queue.

Limitations of Multithreading

- Tracking and switching between the threads consumes memory resources and CPU time, since the state of the threads must be saved while switching.

- Programming with multiple threads is a complex task, since implementing many threads is a challenging task and it is hard to find bugs.

- Since all the threads run in the same process, the threads of a multi-threaded program have access to that process's resources, including global, static and instance fields.

- Synchronization between threads has to be maintained properly to prevent conflicts (like deadlocks) while accessing shared resources such as communication ports and file handles.

Multithreading allows an application to divide a program into independent tasks to make most efficient use of processor's time. However, using multiple threads in an application sometimes reduces the speed of the application. Tracking and switching between multiple threads consumes more CPU time and memory resources. Hence it is not always preferable to use multiple threads in an application.

Maintaining multiple threads is a challenging task as they compete for the shared resources, hence synchronization between multiple threads is a difficult aspect while working with threads. To synchronize the threads in .Net, the Monitor class and lock statements are used.

Chapter 15

Exception Handling in C#

Introduction

The intention of this chapter is to define the concept of exceptions and how to handle them using try, catch and finally keywords. We also look at how to throw exceptions from our own methods using the throw keyword in C#, explain the hierarchy of exceptions, how to define the properties of an exception and how to write our own user defined exception.

Types of Errors

There are two types of errors, namely Compile time errors and Runtime errors. A compile time error happens when the program is getting compiled for execution. It can arise due to multiple factors such as incorrect syntax, an error in the code, a class not found, a loss of precision in data types, etc. They are easy to correct by simply reading the error message associated with the program line number.

A runtime error occurs at the time of program execution and it can't be corrected if it has arisen. Examples include trying to open a file which doesn't exist, divide by zero error, etc. In order to avoid these runtime errors, C# provides exception handling through which the program flow can be controlled so that it doesn't end up in a non-responsive state.

Need for Exception

An example of the need for exception handling is when we are riding our vehicle, we are heading towards a stop signal and we accidentally press the accelerator, instead of holding down the brake. For similar cases in C#, where we may have an exceptional case like a number divided by zero, we could write functions to return error codes. The disadvantage of doing this is that error return codes can be easily ignored and overlooked. When we have no control over error return values, a better mechanism, as provided by .NET Framework's exceptions, is required.

Exceptions integrate well with object oriented languages. When an exception occurs, control is transferred to an appropriate exception handler, which is responsible for recovering from the error condition as shown in Program1

```
int y=0;
try
{
int x=12/y;  ─────────────────┐
x=x+13;                        │
Console.WriteLine("x={0}",x);  │
}                              │
catch {DivideByzeroexception e}│
{                              │
//Handle Exception  ◄──────────┘
}
```

Program1: Sample program to handle exceptions

As trapping and handling of runtime errors is one of the most crucial tasks for any programmer, .NET Framework equips us with exception handling. Exception handling allows you to detect the runtime errors and handle them to avoid the program getting crashed. Instead it shows an exception message providing a reason for the error and what to do next.

Let us understand this with a simple case; the function foreman fetches techies with 3 years of experience. For this, we need to write a code to open the database connection. The code executes fine if the database server is running. The code fails if the database server is not running. Such cases are detected and handled by the .NET Framework.

Class workers
{
        Public void foreman ()
        {

```
        //code to open a database connection
        //get foreman with 3 years' experience
        //display their names
    }
}
```

Program2: Sample program to handle exceptions

Classification of Exception

Exceptions are of two types. They are User-Defined Exceptions and Standard Exceptions as shown in figure1. All user-defined classes derived from System.Exception are User-Defined Exceptions. All pre-defined classes derived from System.Exception are Standard Exceptions. Figure2 shows the hierarchy of standard Exception.

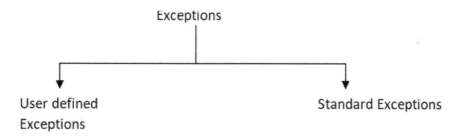

Figure 1: Classification of user-defined and pre-defined Exceptions

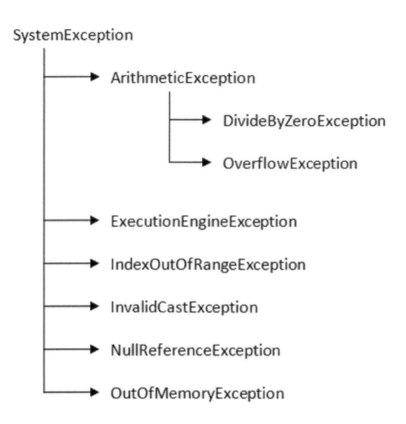

SystemException

ArithmeticException

DivideByZeroException

OverflowException

ExecutionEngineException

IndexOutOfRangeException

InvalidCastException

NullReferenceException

OutOfMemoryException

Figure 2: Classification of SystemException

C# provides an elegant way to handle runtime errors with the help of the try, catch, and finally keywords. The try block contains a code which could throw an exception, and the catch block has the code that handles exceptions. Let us understand this with a simple example.

Here we need to inscribe the block of code that needs to be monitored in the try block. It should be followed by a catch block or finally block. In the try block, the control is transferred to the appropriate catch block and hence "Hi this is Exception Handling" will not be displayed in program3. After executing the catch block the program terminates. The finally block contains code that will be executed irrespective of whether an exception has occurred.

```
using System;
namespace Sample
{
        class sample
        {
                static void Main (string[] args)
                {
                        int a = 0;
                        try
                        {
                                int b = 46 / a;
                                Console.WriteLine ("Hi this is
                                Exception Handling");
                        }
                        catch (DivideByZeroException e)
                        {
                                Console.WriteLine (e);
                        }
                }
        }
}
```

Program3: Handling runtime errors

```
using System;
namespace Sample
{
        class sample
        {
```

```
static void Main (string[] args)
{
        int a = 0;
        int []array = {4, 6};

        try
        {
                int b = 46 / a;
                array[5] = 46;
        }
        catch (DivideByZeroException e)
        {
                Console.WriteLine (e);
        }
catch (IndexOutOfRangeException e)
        {
                Console.WriteLine (e);
        }
    }
  }
}
```

Program4: Handling runtime errors with two catch blocks

The hierarchical relationship enables us to write exception handlers that handle specific errors in a single catch block, without the need to write separate handlers for each exception. In program4 the code has two catch blocks. They can be merged into a single catch block with the super class Exception.

Recollect the hierarchy shown in figure2. In Program5 an IndexOutOfRangeException will be thrown. If the thrown object couldn't find the appropriate catch block, it searches for any other exceptions up in the hierarchy. As there is a catch block with Exception, this block is executed.

```
using System;
namespace Sample
{
        class sample
        {
                static void Main (string[] args)
                {
                        int a = 0;
                        int []array = {4, 6};
                        try
                        {
                                int b = 46 / a;
                                array[5] = 46;
                        }
                        catch (DivideByZeroException e)
                        {
                                Console.WriteLine (e);
                        }
catch (Exception e)
                        {
                                Console.WriteLine (e);
                        }
                }
        }
}
```

Program5: Handling runtime errors using hierarchy of exceptions

The finally block can be used to write termination code that executes in both normal execution as well as exceptional conditions. Let us understand this better with the following code shown in Program6. This is the output of the code, when an exception is thrown.

```
using System;
namespace Sample
{
        class sample
        {
                static void Main (string[] args)
                {
                        int []array = {4, 6};
                        try
                        {
                                array[5] = 23;
                        }
                        catch (IndexOutOfRangeException e)
                        {
                                Console.WriteLine (e);
                        }
                        Finally
                        {
                                Console.WriteLine(" Finally is
executed");
                        }
                }
        }
}
```

Output:

System.IndexOutOfRangeException: Index was outside the bounds of an Array

Finally is executed

Program6: Program and Output when Exception is thrown

```
using System;
namespace Sample
{
        class sample
        {
                static void Main (string[] args)
                {
                        int []array = {4, 6};
                        try
                        {
                                array[0] = 23;
                        }
                        catch (IndexOutOfRangeException e)
                        {
                                Console.WriteLine (e);
                        }
                        Finally
                        {
                                Console.WriteLine(" Finally is
                                executed");
                        }
                }
        }
}
```

Output:

Finally is executed

Program7: Program and Output when Exception is not thrown

This is the output of the code, when an exception is not thrown. As we can see, in the above programs, the output in both the cases is "Finally is executed".

Properties of Exception

Once we get an exception, we need to handle it appropriately. The System.Exception defines properties for every exception. They are Message, StackTrace and InnerException. In program 8, we use the message property and therefore, upon execution, the output is shown at the bottom of program 8.

```
Using System;
namespace Sample
{
        class WithMessage
        {
                Static void Main()
                {
                        try
                        {
                                int a = 5;
                                int b = 0;
                                int c = a / b;
                                Console.WriteLine(c);
                        }
                        catch (DivideByZeroException e)
```

```
            {
                        Console.WriteLine ("Error occurred" +
                        e.Message);
                        Console.Read();
            }
        }
    }
}
```

Output:

Error occurred Attempted to divide by zero

Program8: Exception handling using Message properties

User-Defined Exceptions

User-defined exceptions are exceptions created by a user. User-defined exception classes must inherit from either Exception class or its sub classes. Once we define a user-defined exception, we need to throw it using the throw keyword. That is illustrated best in the example shown in Program9. The block of code where we want the exception to be thrown, is placed in the try block. Explicitly, throw an Exception by creating an instance of the user-defined Exception class. The thrown exception object can be caught in the appropriate catch block. Therefore, upon execution the output is shown below. Note that My Error is displayed because we are calling the base class Constructor using the base keyword.

class MyException: Exception

```csharp
{
        Public MyException (string s): base(s)
        {
        }
}
static void Main()
{
        try
        {
                throw new MyException (" My Error ");
        }
        catch   (MyException e)
        {
                Console.WriteLine (" MyException is thrown {0} ",
                e);
        }
}
```

Output in command prompt:

MyException is thrown

ConsoleApplication1.Sample.sample+Myexception: My Error

Exception Handling Using Defined List of Exceptions

.Net Exception Handling is often a code practice inhibited by a programmer to make application response lenient and informative to user for exception scenarios. As part of this, we handle exceptions based on possible error scenarios during logic processing with proper message displayed to user / logged for later purpose. All these exceptions are handled explicitly one-by-one in the code to cover the possible exceptions scenario. This section covers one of the approaches for exception handling in .net code. It is helpful for readers who would like to make the list of exceptions customizable.

Requirement

Consider a scenario: You receive an error in an application due to some intermittent network issues. There are different list of errors that you observe at various places in the code for which you either want to perform a retry mechanism as these issues are intermittent or throw a custom exception message instead of generic error message to user. The list of exceptions that are causing this issue are identified and can be included in the code to throw a message to the user. However, if you want to include another exception to follow the same message, then you need to modify the code and publish it for release. This section defines the approach to be followed for such instances to avoid code modifications.

Business Context

Due to some intermittent network or access issues, code processing halts by conveying an error message. To provide clean and concise approach for handling exceptions to perform retry or throw a common error message by considering the issues, we can follow the below approach.

Approach

There could be different approaches for handling such requirement. One such approach is detailed below:

- Add an entry to configuration.settings or any configuration file with key/values where value includes list of exceptions comma separated which you would like to handle. For ex:

<setting name = "ExceptionsList" serializeAs = "String">

   <value>
WebException,IOException,UnauthorizedAccessException
</value>

   </setting>

- Make changes to the application code to throw common error message for different set of exception

    o Fetch the list of exceptions from the configuration settings and store in a variable. For ex:

ExceptionsList = ConfigurationVariables.Default.ExceptionsList;

    o Inside the catch block, call method to verify the exception against the defined list

```
public static bool VerifyAgainstExceptionList(string exceptionName,
string listOfExceptions)
    {
        bool isPartOfExceptionList = false;
        string[] exceptions = listOfExceptions.Split(',');
        foreach (string ex in exceptions)
        {
          if (ex.Equals(exceptionName))
```

```
        {
            isPartOfExceptionList = true;
            break ;
        }
    }
    return isPartOfExceptionList;
}
```

- o Throw custom exception (common error) message if the above method returns true.

- In case you want to perform retries on the operation, make the following changes

  - o Include number of retries in config value to make it configurable and store in variable for processing logic

  - o Include while loop to check for retry count

  - o Inside the while loop, for any exception caught, call below method to verify the exception against the defined list

```
if  (VerifyAgainstExceptionList(exceptionName,  listOfExceptions,
retryCount)
{

        ….

// In case of last retry, return false to throw appropriate custom
exception
        if (retryCount == 1)
        {
            return isPartOfExceptionList;
```

```
        }
              ......
}
```

- o Based on number of retry count left, perform retries by reducing the count

- o For the last retry, throw the exception / custom error message to fail the process

The above approach would handle the retry mechanism and custom error message for list of exceptions which we defined. In future, if we want to include any exception for this mechanism, all that we need to do is to add the exception name in config file. This approach can be leverage for any windows and web application.

Thus we have seen with the help of code snippets about handling exceptions with try, catch and finally keywords, hierarchy of exceptions, properties of exceptions and user defined exceptions.

Chapter 16

Reading and Writing in C#

Reading and Writing XML in C#

The System.Xml namespace provides standards-based support for processing XML. The System.Xml namespace contains major XML classes to read and write XML documents. For using XML to store data, we should be familiar with the CRUD techniques to create, read, write, update and delete Xml data.

The reader and writer classes are used to read and write XML documents.

XmlReader Class

This is an abstract class and has methods to read an xml document. Once the XML document is loaded, we can traverse through the nodes for reading information from the XML document.

XmlTextReader Class

This inherits XMLReader and provides methods to read through an XML document.

Example

XmlTextReader reader = new
XmlTextReader("c:\\Test\\Test.xml");

String Test = reader.GetAttribute("test");

In this example we are creating a new instance of XMLtextreader and get the attribute "Test" from the xml.

XMLNode Class

This Class represents a single node of XML documents and has methods to traverse through the nodes of the Document. We can also load and save Xml document using this class.

XMLDocument class

This represents a XML document and on loading a XML Document using XMLDocument class the XML structure is verified internally by the XMLDocument class and throws an exception if the XML is not formed properly.

Example

XmlDocument doc = new XmlDocument();

doc.LoadXml(("<Input type = 'Test' Section = 'B'><Name>Mary</Name></Input>"));

doc.Save("c:\\Test\\Test.xml ");

This Example Creates an XML "test.xml".

XMLNodelist class

This represents a list of nodes of an XMLdocument.

Example

```
XmlNodeList objList = null;
XmlNode objNode = null;
XmlDocument objCurrent;
objCurrent.LoadXml("c:\\Test\\Test.xml");
objList = objCurrent.GetElementsByTagName("A");

if (objList != null)
        {
            for (i = 0; i <= objList.Count - 1; i++)
            {
              objNode = objList.Item(i);
}
}
```

The above code uses XMLnodelist, XMLnode and XMLdocument. The XML is loaded using the string path of an existing XML, in this case test.xml. This can also be done.

Using the objCurrent.Load method which takes Stream, Filename, Textreader, XMLreader as overloaded inputs. Stream contains the Xml document to load.

String Filename which points to the xml for loading, Textreader containing the xml data and XMLreader containing the xml data

XmlWriter Class

This class has methods to write data to XML documents.

Example

```
XmlTextWriter textWriter = new XmlTextWriter
("c:\\Test\\Test.xml", null);

textWriter.WriteStartDocument();

textWriter.WriteComment("Writing comments to the xml file");

textWriter.WriteStartElement("Group");

textWriter.WriteString("Student");

writer.WriteEndElement();

writer.WriteStartElement("AGENT");

writer.WriteAttributeString("LOGIN_NAME", "Mary");

writer.WriteEndElement();

textWriter.WriteStartElement("Char");

textWriter.WriteChars(ch, 0, ch.Length);

textWriter.WriteEndElement();

textWriter.WriteEndDocument();

textWriter.Close();
```

This example creates an xml file, opens it, writes the start tag, writes attributes, characters, string and then closes the xml.

XPathNavigator Class

This Class provides methods to navigate through the xml.

XPathNodeIterator Class

This class provides methods to navigate through the XML nodes.

Example

```
XmlDocument objtest = new XmlDocument("c:\\Test\\Test.xml");
System.Xml.XPath.XPathNavigator objnavi;
System.Xml.XPath.XPathNodeIterator objite;
objnavi = objtest.CreateNavigator();
objite = objnavi.Select("/NewDataSet/Sheet1" + "[" +
index.ToString() + "]" + "/Questions");
objite.MoveNext();
String Test = "";
while (objite.MoveNext())
{
Test = objite.Current.Value;
}
```

This Example navigates through the XML node "Questions".

Modifying an Xml

The ModifyXML function will rename a particular node in the Xml document.

This function takes three input parameters:

xmlPath - The path of the Xml on your machine or server.

nodeToFind -The name of the Node which is to be renamed from the Xml document

nodeOldValue - The node's old Value

nodeNewValue- The node's new Value

```
public void ModifyXML(string xmlPath, string nodeToFind, string
nodeOldVal, string nodeNewValue)
    {
        XmlDocument doc = new XmlDocument();
        doc.Load(@xmlPath);
        XmlNode newXMLNode =
doc.SelectSingleNode("//"+nodeToFind);
        XmlNode
ntest=doc.CreateNode(XmlNodeType.Element,nodeNewValue,"");
        if (newXMLNode.NodeType == XmlNodeType.Element)
        {
            if (newXMLNode.Name == nodeOldVal)

newXMLNode.ParentNode.ReplaceChild(ntest,newXMLNode);
        }
        doc.Save(xmlPath);
    }
```

In the above code, the 'SelectSingleNode' function picks the node which is specified as a parameter and 'ReplaceChild' is a inbuilt .net function which replaces the an xml element name with the text specified as the second parameter.

Example:
```
<?xml version="1.0" encoding="us-ascii"?>
<Projects>
 <Project id="1">
  <User></User>
```

```
    <IBU> </IBU>
    <ProjectCode>BCM</ProjectCode>
    <ProjectDesc>banking</ProjectDesc>
  </Project>
</Projects>
```

In the above Xml, if you want to modify the **User** Child element under **Project** parent element, then call this function as

ModifyXML("C:/abc.xml",User, User, UserName);

Another Scenario can be like this

```
<Projects>
  <Project id="1">
   <User id = "1"></User>
   <User id = "2"></User>
  </Project>
</Projects>
```

Now, if the user wants to modify the User of the user id =2, then the user needs to read the id element also along with the node.

Adding a Parent Node

The function AddParentNode adds a node at the parent level of an Xml document.

Following are the input parameters for this function:

xmlPath- The path of the Xml on your machine or server.

parentNode-The name of the node which you want to create.

```
public void AddParentNode(string xmlPath, string parentNode)
   {
     XmlDocument doc = new XmlDocument();
     XmlNode node;
     if (File.Exists(xmlPath))
     {
        doc.Load(xmlPath);
        XmlElement product = doc.CreateElement(parentNode);
        doc.DocumentElement.InsertAfter(product,doc.DocumentElemen
        t.LastChild);
doc.Save(xmlPath);
        }
   }
```

In the above code, the InsertAfter method which is a .net inbuilt function inserts the specified node immediately after the specified reference node.

Example:

```
<?xml version = "1.0" encoding = "us-ascii"?>
<Projects>
  <Project id = "1">
    <IBU> </IBU>
    <ProjectCode>BCM</ProjectCode>
    <ProjectDesc>banking</ProjectDesc>
  </Project>
  <User>
  </User>
</Projects>
```

In the above Xml, if you want to add the **User** as a parent element, then call this function as

AddParentNode("c:/abc.xml", User);

Creating a Child Node below a particular Parent Node

While working with Xml, the requirement comes to create a child node below a particular Parent Node. This is where this function CreateChild can become handy. Following are the input parameters for this function:

strXmlPath - The path of the xml on your machine or server.

parentNode -The Node after which you want to place your node.

childNode -The name of the child Node.

```
public void AddChildNode(string strXmlPath, string parentNode,
string childNode)
   {
     XmlDocument doc = new XmlDocument();
     XmlNode node;
     if (File.Exists(strXmlPath))
     {
        doc.Load(xmlPath);
        XmlNode xmlNodeList1 = doc.SelectSingleNode("//" +
        childNode);
        XmlNode xmlNodeList2 = doc.SelectSingleNode("//" +
        parentNode);
        if (xmlNodeList1 != null)
        {
        //Display the message that the Parent node already contains a
        child node with the same name.
```

```
        }
        else
        {
            node = doc.CreateElement(childNode);
            xmlNodeList2.AppendChild(node);
        }
        }
        doc.Save(strXmlPath);
    }
```

Example:

```
<?xml version = "1.0" encoding = "us-ascii"?>
<Projects>
  <Project id = "1">
   <User></User>
   <IBU> </IBU>
   <ProjectCode>BCM</ProjectCode>
   <ProjectDesc>banking</ProjectDesc>
  </Project>
</Projects>
```

In the above Xml, if you want to add the **User** Child element under **Project** parent element, then call this function as

AddChildNode("C:/abc.xml",Project,User);

Getting a Particular Node from a Xml document

The GetRequiredNode function returns the name of the node you require in the form of a string from your xml document. Following are the input parameters for this function:

strXmlPath- The path of the Xml on your machine or server.

parentNode-The Node after which you want to place your node.

childNode-The name of the child Node.

```
public string GetRequiredNode(string strXmlPath, string nodeToFind)
    {
        XmlDocument doc = new XmlDocument();
        if (File.Exists(strXmlPath))
        {
            doc.Load(xmlPath);
            XmlTextReader textReader = new
            XmlTextReader(strXmlPath);
            // Read until end of file
            while (textReader.Read())
            {
                XmlNodeType nType = textReader.NodeType;
                if (nType == XmlNodeType.Element)
                {
                    if (textReader.Name.ToString() == nodeToFind)
                    {
                        string strNode= textReader.Name.ToString();
                        textReader.Close();
                        return strNode;
                    }
                }
            }
        }
        return null;
    }
```

Example:

```
<?xml version = "1.0" encoding = "us-ascii"?>
<Projects>
 <Project id = "1">
  <IBU> </IBU>
  <ProjectCode>BCM</ProjectCode>
  <ProjectDesc>banking</ProjectDesc>
 </Project>
</Projects>
```

In the above Xml, if you want to get the **IBU** element, then call this function as

GetRequiredNode("C:/abc.xml", IBU);

Uploading and Reading Excel Sheet in C#

Introduction

Sometimes we come across situation where we need to upload an excel sheet, read the data from that file using C# and display it on our web page. In such situations, instead of saving the data of the excel sheet into database and establishing a connection to read that data, we can directly read the data from excel sheet.

An Example:

In this example we are providing the user with the functionality to upload a file. The code checks whether the uploaded file is an excel sheet or not. After successful validation, the file is saved at the specified location and later used to display its data on a web page. The example can be explained in following steps:

Steps

1. Create an excel sheet.

2. Create a web page that has the functionality to upload excel sheet.

3. Upload the excel sheet at a specified location.

4. Create another web page that reads the excel sheet and displays the data in tabular format.

Step 1:

Consider the example of an excel sheet that consists of employee details with the following data.

EmployeeID	EmployeeName	JobLevel
1	XYZ	3
2	ABC	3
3	PQR	3

Save this excel sheet at some location in your system.

Step 2:

Create a web page that contains a FileUpload control that is used to upload a file.

Below is the screenshot of a sample webpage.

Select an ExcelSheet To be Uploaded   Browse...

Upload File

Step 3:

On a click of the "Upload File" button, perform the following functionality:

```
protected void UploadExcel_Click (object sender, EventArgs e)
{
    string fname = FileUpload1.FileName;
    string fpath = Server.MapPath ("~/reports/" + fname); // here
    "reports" is the name of the folder where the excel sheet is to be
    saved
    string extension = System.IO.Path.GetExtension(fname);
    if (FileUpload1.PostedFile != null &&
    FileUpload1.PostedFile.FileName != "")   // to check whether or
    not user has selected any file to be uploaded
    {
    if ((extension == ".xls" || extension == ".xlsx"))// to check whether the
        file to be uploaded is an excel sheet or not
        {
            FileUpload1.SaveAs(fpath);
            Page.ClientScript.RegisterClientScriptBlock(typeof(Page),
    "Alert", "alert('Report uploaded successfully.')", true);
        }
        else
        {
```

212

```
        Page.ClientScript.RegisterClientScriptBlock(typeof(Page),
        "Alert", "alert('The file you are trying  to upload is not an
        excel file')", true);
        }
}
else
    {
        Page.ClientScript.RegisterClientScriptBlock(typeof(Page),
        "Alert", "alert('Kindly select a file to be uploaded.')", true);
    }
}
```

On a click of the Browse button, the user is asked to select a file from a particular location.

Once the user selects a file and clicks on Upload File button, the following validations are performed:

1. Whether or not user has selected a file to be uploaded.

2. Whether or not the selected file is an excel sheet (extension .xls or .xlsx)

After proper validation, the file is saved at the specified location. Here, in this example, "reports" is the name of the folder in which excel sheets are saved.

Step 4:

This step involves creation of a web page that reads the uploaded excel sheet and displays the data of the excel sheet in a tabular format.

For this we need to include the following namespaces in our C# file: "**_System.Data.OleDb_**", "**_System.Data_**".

Declare the following variables as public and global variables:

```
public int[] id = new int[10];
public string[] name = new string[10];
public int[] jl = new int[10];
public int d;
```

At Page Load Event write the following code:

```
string path = Server.MapPath(@"reports/kshop.xls");
OleDbConnection oledbConn = new OleDbConnection
("Provider=Microsoft.Jet.OLEDB.4.0;Data Source='" + path + "';
Extended Properties=Excel 8.0");
OleDbCommand cmd = new OleDbCommand();
OleDbDataAdapter oleda = new OleDbDataAdapter();
DataSet ds = new DataSet();
oledbConn.Open();
cmd.CommandText = "SELECT * FROM [Sheet1$] ";
cmd.Connection = oledbConn;
oleda.SelectCommand = cmd;
oleda.Fill(ds);
oledbConn.Close();
d = ds.Tables[0].Rows.Count;
int i = 0;
while (d > 0 && i < d)
{
        id[i] = Int32.Parse(ds.Tables[0].Rows[i][0].ToString());
        name[i] = (string)ds.Tables[0].Rows[i][1];
        jl[i] = Int32.Parse(ds.Tables[0].Rows[i][2].ToString());
        i++;
}
```

Here "reports/kshop.xls" is the path of the excel sheet that is to be read.

Now to display the data in tabular format. Write the following code in your source file:

```
<body>
   <form id = "form1" runat = "server">
   <div>
   <h4 align = "center"> DETAILS OF EMPLOYEE </h4>
<table border = "2" width = "60%" align = "center" bgcolor =
"#CCCCCC"> <tr><th>EmpID</th>
<th> Employee Name </th>
<th>Job Level</th>
</tr>
   <%for (int i = 0; i < d; i++){ %>
       <tr><td align = "center"><% = id[i] %></td>
       <td align = "center"><% = name[i]%></td>
       <td align = "center"><% = jl[i] %></td>
</tr><%} %>
   </table>
   </div>
   </form>
</body>
```

A table with all the data from the excel sheet is displayed once the webpage is browsed.

Below is the screenshot of the result of the above code.

DETAILS OF EMPLOYEE

EmpID	Employee Name	Job Level
1	XYZ	3
2	ABC	3
3	PQR	3

Chapter 17

C# - Coding Standards, Naming Conventions and Best Practices

This document focuses on the rules and principles that a programmer should follow while writing application in C#. Every organization will have its own naming convention standards. This document provides the best practices and naming conventions for C#, and they are consistent with Microsoft .Net Framework and are easy to read. The document also provides the C# syntaxes for various connection strings. By using these standards, we can make sure that any other developer who is reading our code can easily understand all the logic of the program without any issues. This reduces the time required for project transition in big projects.

Naming Conventions

Type	Naming Convention	Example
Classes	PascalCasing, no Underscores	public class TestClass { //.. }
Methods	PascalCasing, no Underscores	public void TestMethod1() { //.. }
Namespaces	PascalCasing, no Underscores	Test.ContinuousDevelopment.Cod ingStandards
Struct	PascalCasing, no Underscores	struct SimpleStruct { //.. }
Method Arguments	camelCasing	public void Add(LogEvent logEvents) { // ... }
Enums	PascalCasing,	Enum Test { // ... }
Properties	PascalCasing	Public string AddValues {get; set;}
Assemblies	PascalCasing	Test.ContinuousDevelopment.Cod ingStandards.dll
Delegate Classes	PascalCasing, Add Delegate at the end of the name	public class SampleDelegate { //.. }
Delegates	camelCasing	public delegate String myMethodDelegate(int myInt);
Exception Classes	PascalCasing, Add Exception at the end of the name	public class InvalidAdditionException { //.. }

Local Variables	camelCasing	int itemCount;
Interfaces	PascalCasing, no Underscores. Start the name with "I"	Public interface IemployeeDetails { //.. }
Global Variables	camelCasing	int recordCount;
Class level private variables	camelCasing, use Underscore	int _employeeName;
Constants (Used Publicly)	PascalCasing	Public const string EmployeeName="test";
Constants (Private to a function)	CamelCasing	Public const string employeeName="test";

Best Practices

Below are mentioned some of the practices that can be incorporated while coding. These practices will make the code more readable and robust. These are just the best practices and not the mandatory ones. But if you follow them, it will help you in keeping your code clean and readable.

- Keep the classes and files short and do not include more than 2000 lines per class. Do not put too many big comments which will increase your overall lines in the class.

- Don't include more than one class in a single file. Put each class in separate files. This is the best practice while creating classes.

- When an expression or statement is too long to fit in a single line, break it into two or more lines depending on the length of the expression. This helps in easy code reading.

  e.g.: int val = (a1 * b1 / (c1 – d1 + e1) +
  (f1 * g1)) + 100;

- Use "///" for documentation comments

- Avoid Hungarian notations as

  e.g.: int iCounter; // Declare as itemCount
  string strEmployeeName; // Declare as employeeName

- Avoid using capitals for constants and read-only variables

  e.g.: public static const string EMPLOYEENAME = "name1";
  // Declare as EmployeeName

- Avoid using abbreviations

  e.g.: InformationGroup infGrp;
  // Declare as informationGroup instead on infGrp

- Declare one variable per line. This technique will be helpful during commenting the variables.

  e.g.: int itemCount1; // Avoid – int itemCount1, itemCount2;

- Use meaningful names for classes, methods etc.

  e.g.: public class EmployeeDetails; // Avoid – public class A;

- Avoid using uppermost parenthesis for "return" statements.

  e.g.: return (a + b) / 2; // Avoid – return ((a + b) / 2);

- Include blank lines between methods, properties etc. as they will increase the readability.

- Use predefined names instead of system types

  e.g.: int itemCount; // Avoid -- Int32 itemCount;
       string itemName; // Avoid – String itemName;

- Do not suffix Enum name with "Enum" word as it is consistent with MS .Net framework consistent with prior rule of no type indicators in identifiers.

- Use singular names for Enums because it is consistent with the Microsoft's .NET Framework and makes the code more natural to read.

- Declare all members at top of class as it is generally accepted practice that prevents the need to hunt for variable declarations.

  e.g.:
       public class Employee
       {
            public static string EmployeeName;
            public string EmployeeNumber {get; set;}
            public DateTime DateJoined {get; set;}
            public DateTime DateConfirmed {get; set;}
            public decimal Salary {get; set;}

```
            // Constructor
            public Employee ()  {      // ...  }
     }
```

- Namespaces should have clearly defined structures.

  e.g.:
  namespace Company.Product.Module.SubModule

- Use implicit type "var" for local variable declaration as it will remove the clutter.

  e.g.:
  var stream = File.Save(path);

- Avoid using Underscores in identifiers as it is consistent with the Microsoft's .NET Framework and makes code more natural to read.

  e.g.:
  public DateTime date_Joined; // Declare as -- public DateTime dateJoined;

- Avoid hard coding numbers. Use constants if the value is likely to change.

Connection Strings

This section provides the various connection strings, in C#, that can be used to connect to SQL Server, Excel and MS.

Database	Type of Connection	Connection String

Microsoft SQL Server	ODBC – Standard Connection	OdbcConnection conn = new OdbcConnection();
		conn.ConnectionString =
		    "Driver = {SQL Server};" +
		    "Server = ServerName;" +
		    "DataBase = DataBaseName;" +
		    "Uid = UserName;" +
		    "Pwd = Password;";

Microsoft SQL Server	ODBC – Trusted Connection	OdbcConnection conn = new OdbcConnection();
		conn.ConnectionString =
		    "Driver = {SQL Server};" +
		    "Server = ServerName;" +
		    "DataBase = DataBaseName;" +
		    "Trusted_Connection = Yes;";

Microsoft SQL Server	Oledb – Standard Connection	OleDbConnection conn = new OleDbConnection();
		conn.ConnectionString =
		    "Driver = SQLOLEDB;" +
		    "Data Source = ServerName;" +
		    "Initial Catalog = DataBaseName;" +
		    "User id = UserName;" +
		    "Password = Password;";

Microsoft SQL Server	Oledb – Trusted Connection	OleDbConnection conn = new OleDbConnection();
		conn.ConnectionString =
		    "Driver = SQLOLEDB;" +
		    "Data Source = ServerName;" +
		    "Initial Catalog = DataBaseName;" +
		    "Integrated Security = SSPI;";

Microsoft SQL Server	.Net DataProvider - Standard Connection	SqlConnection conn = new SqlDbConnection(); conn.ConnectionString = "Data Source =

		ServerName;" +
		    "Initial Catalog =
		DataBaseName;" +
		    "User id = UserName;" +
		    "Password = Password;";

Microsoft
SQL Server
	.Net DataProvider -
	Trusted Connection
		SqlConnection conn = new
		SqlConnection();
		conn.ConnectionString =
		    "Data Source =
		ServerName;" +
		    "Initial Catalog =
		DataBaseName;" +
		    "Integrated Security =
		SSPI;";

Microsoft
SQL Server
	.Net DataProvider
	– Using IP Address
		SqlConnection conn = new
		SqlConnection();
		conn.ConnectionString =
		    "Network Library =
		DBMSSOCN;" +
		    "Data Source =
		xxx.xxx.xxx.xxx,1433;" +
		    "Initial Catalog =
		DataBaseName;" +
		    "User Id = UserName;" +
		    "Password = Password;";

Excel	ODBC DSN	OdbcConnection conn = new
		OdbcConnection();
		conn.ConnectionString =
		    "Dsn = DsnName;" +
		    "Uid = UserName;" +
		    "Pwd = Password;";

Excel	ODBC without
	DSN
		OdbcConnection conn = new
		OdbcConnection();
		conn.ConnectionString =
		    "Driver = {Microsoft Excel
		Driver (*.xls)};" +
		    "Driverid = 790;" +
		    "Dbq =
		C:\MyPath\SpreadSheet.xls;" +
		    "DefaultDir = C:\MyPath;";

Microsoft Access	ODBC DSN	OdbcConnection conn = new OdbcConnection(); conn.ConnectionString = "Dsn=DsnName";

Microsoft Access	ODBC – standard security	OdbcConnection conn = new OdbcConnection();
		conn.ConnectionString =
		   "Driver = {Microsoft Access Driver (*.mdb)};" +
		   "Dbq = c:\myPath\myDb.mdb;" +
		   "Uid = Admin; Pwd = ;";

Microsoft Access	ODBC – Work Group	OdbcConnection conn = new OdbcConnection();
		conn.ConnectionString =
		   "Driver = {Microsoft Access Driver (*.mdb)};" +
		   "Dbq = c:\myPath\myDb.mdb;" +
		   "SystemDb = c:\myPath\myDb.mdw;";

Microsoft Access	Oledb with MS jet – standard security	OleDbConnection conn = new OleDbConnection();
		conn.ConnectionString =
		   "Provider = Microsoft.Jet.OLEDB.4.0;" +
		   "Data Source = c:\mypath\myDb.mdb;" +
		   "User id = admin;" +
		   "Password = ";

Microsoft Access	Oledb with MS jet – Work Group	OleDbConnection conn = new OleDbConnection();
		conn.ConnectionString =
		   "Provider = Microsoft.Jet.OLEDB.4.0;" +
		   "Data Source = c:\mypath\myDb.mdb;" +
		   "System Database = c:\mypath\myDb.mdw;";

Microsoft Access	Oledb with MS jet – With password	OleDbConnection conn = new OleDbConnection();
		conn.ConnectionString =
		   "Provider = Microsoft.Jet.OLEDB.4.0;" +
		   "Data Source = c:\mypath\myDb.mdb;" +
		   "Database Password = Password;"

Chapter 18

Code Refactoring

Code refactoring is essentially the process of changing or restructuring an existing piece of code and to tailor the same without affecting its functionality or the external behavior. The objective of code refactoring is to change the internal structure of an existing body of code using a disciplined technique without altering its functional behavior so that the code becomes more maintainable by becoming more readable and with reduced complexity and higher extensibility.

Thus, the advantages of code refactoring include better readability, reduced complexity, enhanced maintainability and improved extensibility owing to more expressive internal architecture and object model. Hence, the process of refactoring intends to improve the overall structure of a program by incorporating or adhering to the OOP best practices, boost its performance, and increase its readability which in turn makes it easier to maintain the code. The overall exercise yields a code which is better and yet adheres to the intended functionality.

The overall structure of the code gets improved when code refactoring comes into play. The transformation or code refactoring in other words is taken up in a piece-meal approach/fashion. And since each transformation is small and targets small fragments of code thus it is less likely to go wrong and is not prone to errors. The entire process adopts an approach wherein we have an iterative cycle which consists of small blocks of code transformation. And after making the transformation unit testing is performed to ensure the correctness of the change before moving ahead with the next transformation. Therefore, even though each transformation does little, but a sequence of transformations can result in significant restructuring and lead to more manageable and well-structured code.

However, having the presence of strong unit tests in place is recommended so that each transformation or refactoring can be validated to ensure that the external/functional behavior of the module is correct and has not been altered inadvertently by the refactoring exercise. This way it helps the programmer to revert back the small change in case of failure of the unit test. Additionally, the change can be tried or implemented on different lines altogether in case the functionality gets broken.

Thus, the objective of refactoring is that external behavior of the system does not get broken and at the same time the internal structure undergoes refinement and thereby results in better readability, increased maintainability and extensibility of the software program.

Why Refactoring?

Refactoring is required in order to maintain the correct naming conventions for variables, proper indentation of the statements, formatting of the code, enhancing the readability for other coders. Such changes made effectively lead to enhancement of the overall quality parameter of the deliverable and make the application more stable, as fix for a defect has to be applied at one single place or piece of code rather than searching for similar code in other modules which is otherwise susceptible to error owing to reason that changes to few other methods may get omitted inadvertently.

Tool-based refactoring is intended for automating this tedious and tiresome manual process thereby making developers much more productive and at the same time it results in a code base which has higher quality.

Refactoring Techniques in Visual Studio

Refactoring may involve lot of manual work and usually it is a manual way of removing errors, but it doesn't guarantee 100% accuracy as some mistakes gets passed here. The search and replace features of the code editor come to our aid here. These features not only curtail on the extent of laborious manual work involved in refactoring but also ensure the correctness of the unit of work.

Whereas manual work in refactoring such as even search and replace can be tiresome, cumbersome and tedious at the same time it is more prone to errors and likely to result in functionality failure or to a broken system. Thanks to the inbuilt out of the box features of Visual Studio which are helpful in employing the various refactoring techniques.

Visual Studio 2005/2008 and onwards editions support the below refactoring techniques:

- Extract Method

- Rename

- Extract Interface

- Encapsulate Field

- Reorder Parameters

- Remove Parameters

- Promote Local Variable to Parameter

To use these features just highlight the relevant piece of code as applicable and then right click → choose/select a specific feature (as shown below)

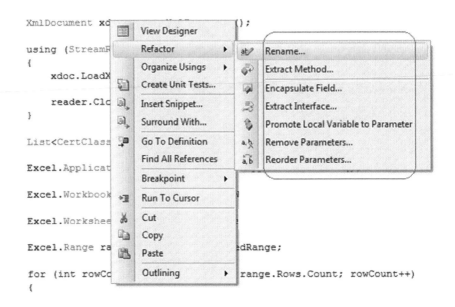

Rename

This operation is one of the simplest refactoring techniques which involve the ability to change the name of a variable (Class, Struct or Field etc.) and also update all the occurrences and references made to the field in question within its scope.

To use, just highlight the variable name that you want to change, right click, and select Refactor → Rename. Subsequently, a client form for the new name will appear (as shown in below picture) and changes can be previewed for all the references to the variable being renamed, before the actual implementation of the changes/update.

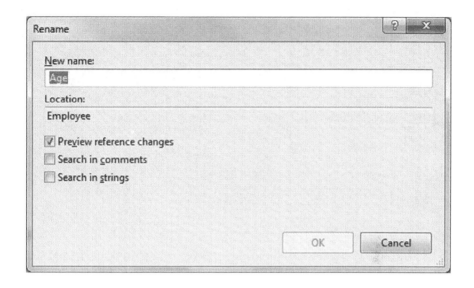

At times it happens that after a bit of thought, you decide that some other variable name is more fitting name for the type in question. Rather than having to make use of manual find/replace techniques, the Rename refactoring reliably renames all the occurrences of the selected token throughout the entire references to the same variable.

Extract Method

Using Extract Method refactoring technique, the required lines of code of an existing method can be extracted and ported to create a new method from it. This is done by selecting the required lines from an existing method and choosing Refactor → Extract method from the context menu. A new method gets created with the selected lines of code moved to this newly created method. Additionally, the selected lines of code in the existing method will be replaced by a call to the new method created.

A dialog box is presented which allows entering a name of the new method to be generated (see below figure). Additionally, the new method is automatically defined as private and static, as the code statements did not refer to any instance level variables (generally speaking, extracted methods will be given the most restrictive modifiers possible).

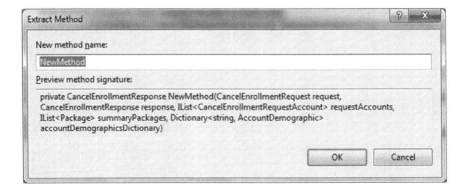

Additionally, from longer routines we can extract more than one subroutines. Similarly, for identical routines, we can remove the duplicate ones and in their place a common function can be utilized.

This also enhances the overall quality of an application as a bug fix can be applied at a central place rather than searching for similar code in other modules, which otherwise makes the program more prone to errors thereby impairing the overall quality parameter of the deliverable.

Encapsulate Field

It is a very useful feature for generating the property of a member. We can use it to encapsulate the public data members as well as for exposing the private data members. Here is an example where we will be exposing the _age variable.

```
public class Employee
{
    int _age;
}
```

To use, just highlight the private member name and right click, select Refactor → Encapsulate Field. A dialog box will appear as shown hereunder. This would have one text field to capture the name of the property which is used to encapsulate the private field/member.

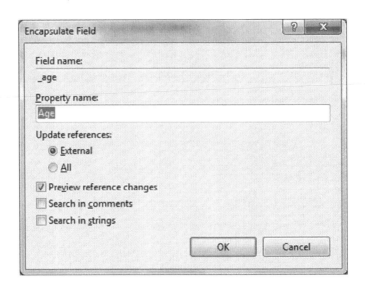

Visual Studio 2005/2008 automates the process using the Encapsulate Field refactoring. Place the cursor on _age and select Encapsulate Field from the Refactor menu. This brings up the Encapsulate Field dialog box which accepts the name of the public property to expose this private member. The Encapsulate Field will also omit the prefix such as underscore '_' of the private member when suggesting a property name. Thus, select any field which is a private and activate the refactoring of interest which results in creation of a property wrapping the private member.

Extract Interface

It will create the definition of the interface from the public methods present in the class. When multiple classes or structs have a set of members which are common, it would be better if the common code is moved to an interface and it is always useful to have these members within an interface and make the classes or structs derive

234

from this interface. This will make the code more readable and manageable. The Extract Interface refactoring technique allows us to create a new interface with members from an existing class or struct.

To use, just highlight the class name and right click, select Refactor → Extract Interface. A screen appears as shown below which makes it possible to make selection of the properties/methods or members to be included as definition of the public interface.

For this, all we have to do is select the methods/members we want to move to an interface and choose Refactor → Extract Interface from the context menu. This would result in a popup dialog box.

Additionally, you can provide a file name in the dialog. This gives you the capability to automatically generate interfaces based on an existing class or struct definition.

Promote Local Variable to Parameter

When you are constructing a method, you may find that a set of local variables would be better suited as arguments provided by the caller. Even at times when we are defining a method, we may find that it will be better to move some of the local variables in the method to the parameters of the method so that the method becomes more generic. Thus, Promote Local Variable to Parameter refactoring technique allows us to move a local variable in a method as a parameter to the method.

For this, all we have to do is select the variable we would like to promote as parameter and choose Refactoring → Promote Local Variable To Parameter from the context menu. This change will not only promote the local variable as parameter but also update all the references to the method with the new parameter.

It simply lets you select a local variable and make it a parameter with just a single click.

Remove Parameters

The Remove Parameters refactoring is more or less self-explanatory. As the name suggests the Remove Parameter refactoring technique allows us to remove parameters from a method's signature. If we want an argument to be removed from a method, all we have to do is place cursor within the method and select Refactor → Remove parameter from the context menu. This will open a popup dialog box prompting the user to select the parameters for removal. This refactoring technique will not only remove the parameter but also update all the references to the method.

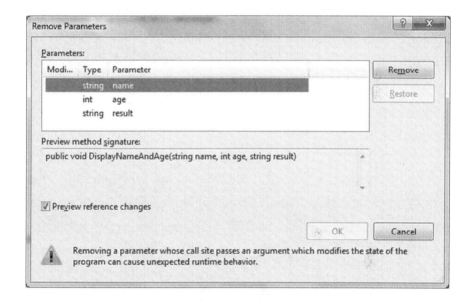

Thus, this refactoring technique allows us to change the signature of a method by removing parameters. However, you cannot change the method return type. You can change the signatures of methods, indexers, as well as constructors. However, it is especially important to review the result of this refactoring, given that this affects each and every invocation of the method.

Reorder Parameters

As you would expect, this refactoring allows you to change the ordering of a member's arguments. It provides you the ability to substitute the signature of a method by changing the order of parameters. As the name suggests the Reorder Parameters refactoring technique allows us to change parameter orders in a method. In order to change the position of parameters all we have to do is to place the cursor within the method and choose Refactor → Reorder Parameters from the context menu. This will open a popup dialog box which has provision for changing the order or parameters.

The Reorder Parameters refactoring technique not only changes the order of parameters but has also updates all the references. Refer to the screen shot below which depicts a screen/dialog where input parameters of the method namely "DisplayNameAndAge" being reordered.

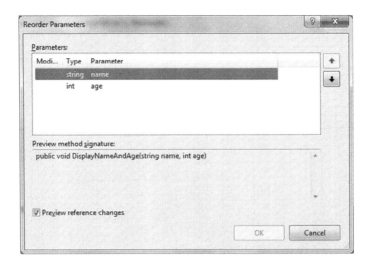

Especially the asymmetric nature of the overloaded methods may be confusing (or at very least annoying) to the object user. Thus, using reorder parameters refactoring, you can quickly clean up the existing model for such a scenario.

The above cited features are indeed very useful and could boost your programming time just like code snippets. These Refactoring operations that are being introduced would lessen the chance of bugs appearing whenever we want to reorganize our code. So I guess it's a very good practice to make use of these tools whenever you want to clean-out your code. And overall this activity has manifold advantage(s) which yields a better code in terms of readability, quality, overall design, maintainability and extensibility.

References

1. http://msdn.microsoft.com/en-us/library/512aeb7t.aspx

2. https://msdn.microsoft.com

3. http://www.devx.com/dotnet/Article/7003

Made in the USA
Monee, IL
25 February 2020

22314866R00138